GLASS NEEDLES & GOOSE QUILLS

GLASS NEEDLES & GOOSE QUILLS

ELEMENTARY LESSONS IN ATOMIC PROPERTIES, NUCLEAR FAMILIES & RADICAL POETICS

LISSA KIERNAN

Haley's
Athol, Massachusetts

Haley's
488 South Main Street
Athol, MA 01331
haley.antique@verizon.net
800.215.8805

Cover art by Stephen MacLellan.
Copy edited by Lauren Thomas.
Proof read by Cindy Hochman of "100 Proof" Copyediting Services.

Library of Congress Control Number: 2016951906

Kiernan, Lissa.
    Poems. Selections.
    Glass needles & goose quills / Lissa Kiernan.
    Athol, MA : Haley's, [2018]
    120 pages / 15.24x22.86 cm
    Includes bibliographical references.
    1. American poetry--21st century. 2. Yankee Atomic Power Plant (Mass.)--Poetry. 3. Brain--Tumors--Patients--Biography. 4. Fathers and daughters--Massachusetts--Berkshire County. I. Title.
    ISBN 978-0-9916102-8-0 (trade paperback)
    ISBN 978-0-9967730-0-3 (eBook)
    PS3611.I44555 A6 2016

For the poets, physicians, physicists, and sacrifice communities everywhere.

And for my father.

Contents

Drawn in by a Backstory
    a foreword by Jane Gagliardi ix

Exploring and Asserting Poetry's Unique Ability to
    Document and Re-Vision the Nuclear Age
       an introduction by Lissa Kiernan 1

Glass Needles 5

Half-Life 59

Goose Quills 65

About the Author 93

Acknowledgments 95

Comments on the Text 97

Permissions 99

Resources and Works Cited 101

Drawn in by a Backstory

a foreword by Jane Gagliardi, MD, MHS
Associate Professor of Psychiatry & Behavioral Sciences and of Medicine
Duke University School of Medicine

My mother asked me almost offhandedly one day if I would be willing to look at Lissa Kiernan's manuscript for accuracy/plausibility of medical details. It had been decades since I had interacted with any of the Kiernan family. I did not know what sort of medical issues I would be reviewing, but I agreed. I quickly assessed the medical descriptions as sufficient. I found myself drawn in by a backstory I had never considered about a family I had known, but I was riveted by the narrative provided by a daughter with complicated emotions surrounding her father's illness and death.

I started piano lessons with Mrs. (Claudette) Kiernan, Lissa Kiernan's mother, when I was four years old. They lived in North Orange, close to my home in Tully, Massachusetts. My mother, Marcia Gagliardi (also a student of Mrs. Kiernan's), taught English to local high school students later to include Lissa Kiernan, who also babysat my sisters and me from time to time.

Mrs. Kiernan moved from North Orange to Amherst, Massachusetts, when I was nine or ten, but I continued to take piano lessons from her on Tuesday evenings despite the associated ninety-minute round-trip commute. I recall there was no Mr. Kiernan, but I never knew why. Mrs. Kiernan was an exacting piano teacher who was sparing in her use of praise. The Kiernan sisters were talented and musical, and I often heard Lissa and her sisters practicing their woodwind instruments upstairs during my lessons. I'm sure my admiration of their prowess inspired my fourth-grade choice of the clarinet as my second instrument.

Throughout my childhood, the largest piece of artwork in our house was a poster my mother had carefully mounted and framed, displayed prominently in the kitchen. An illustration of the dandelion life cycle was depicted with the following poem.

I want to die a natural death
like the dandelion seeding in the fall,
followed by growing in the spring . . .
I want us to go on.
I want us simply to go on.

—Marie Cartier

Block letters at the bottom of the poster read DISARMAMENT NOW.

One summer my family visited a few nuclear reactors, including by hiking through the woods to Pilgrim Power Plant in Plymouth, Massachusetts. Not only was I unenthusiastic about the requisite trespassing, I also was terrified of radioactive exposure and its potential effects on my body.

Later, my mother acquired an architectural rendition of "Meltdown Mall," a foam-mounted poster by Provincetown artist Jay Critchley with an illustrated cutaway of a nuclear reactor and tongue-in-cheek stores and attractions. It stayed in the room where I diligently practiced piano in hopes of meeting Mrs. Kiernan's standards.

I resonate with Lissa's memoir on multiple levels. As a child of the 1980s who was terrified of nuclear anything, I understand her fear. As the daughter of the anti-nuclear protester and editor/publisher of this book, I "get it" even though I can't rationally explain why. As an academic physician-educator, I appreciate challenges in establishing causal associations with retrospective data (and am skeptical about many claims of harm). As an internist-psychiatrist, I have witnessed a wide spectrum of human behavior and reactions to acute, chronic, life-limiting, life-altering, and terminal illness including at the very end of life.

I frequently remind my mother that she, and other activists, should endeavor to expand their audience with evidence-based and compelling arguments. Lissa Kiernan's memoir is not a scientific manuscript. Her report may not satisfy the Bradford Hill criteria for establishing causality, but her argument may promote more careful scrutiny of possible harmful effects of radioactivity. The human aspects of the story, written by a musically-accomplished, talented poet and devoted daughter, are likely to compel—and may move some to action.

Exploring and Asserting Poetry's Unique Ability to Document and Re-Vision the Nuclear Age

an introduction by Lissa Kiernan

Glass Needles & Goose Quills charts the rise and fall-out surrounding the operation of Yankee Rowe Atomic—a prototype for President Dwight D. Eisenhower's Atoms for Peace program—alongside my experiences caring for my father during his illness with brain cancer and my contemplation of nuclearism's place in the poetic canon. The long-form braided essay is an eruption of associations, including reportage, documentary poems, and memoir, a form that somehow managed to take up the messy strands of my disparate concerns and plait them into some semblance of order, even one that continuously threatened to unravel where personal and industrial meltdowns converge.

Using poetry both as a mechanism to bring evidence into the room and as a means of reclaiming voice in the wake of disaster, *Glass Needles & Goose Quills* also serves as a companion to my full-length poetry collection, *Two Faint Lines in the Violet* published by Negative Capability Press. *Glass Needles & Goose Quills* explicates a number of poems in that volume while continuing to explore and assert poetry's unique ability to document and re-vision the nuclear age by illustrating how, when probing somewhere between the personal and political—if we observe closely—we may uncover the social.

With the conversation on climate crisis nearing a perfect storm, the time has come to contemplate at what cost we persist in inviting nuclear energy technology into our lives and to question whether lessons learned will be heeded. It is my hope that *Glass Needles & Goose Quills* contributes to the conversation (even or perhaps especially because, it is told through the lens of a layperson who felt wholly unequipped to be this story's reporter) by examining how things leak into each other, whether by accident or design, and how power, in all definitions of the word, has profound implications on every aspect of our lives.

While I gave careful attention to unearthing the complicated truths of Yankee Rowe's history as objectively and accurately as possible, memory, personal and collective, is always short-circuited by various circumstantial and psychological interferences even as it aspires to be a good conductor of electrical current, one giving as little resistance as possible to the flow of energy—even as it aspires to rise to the level of poetry.

GLASS NEEDLES

Glass Needles

The summer my father was diagnosed with a brain tumor, a Rose of Sharon seeded itself in my Brooklyn backyard. The yard's previous caretakers had tried to make the most of the narrow swath of rocky dirt, laying in a spruce set too far back and now leaning like a famous tower to one side; two hosta, one of which thrived; a crabapple tree half-dead from a battle with Asian long-horned beetles; and the prize: a hydrangea whose petals faded into papery blues and bruised purples at harvest time.

The Rose of Sharon had chosen a spot behind the spruce, where I worried it would not get enough light. Still, it was new life, and I wanted to interpret it as a sign that my father would survive. As a poet, I'm big on semiotics. I look for signs everywhere, both those less obvious—a clock chiming in convergence with some seemingly random event—and those hidden in plain sight—words pulled from billboard signage observed during my workday commute.

I have a passing, pedestrian interest in augury, too, especially the ancient art of divination by observing the behavior of birds, though augury's popularity grew to include the study of bears, snakes, and other animals thought to be sacred to the gods, as well as natural phenomena like lightning and thunder, and even the analysis of some man-made objects: the creaking of floorboards, the breaking of mirrors, the trajectory of arrows, of hurled knives.

In ancient Rome, some lucky high official's job would be to interpret the will of the gods by studying birds in flight: whether they flew in flocks or alone; what songs they sang; what shapes they formed. "Taking the auspices" was not so much a sign of something to come as a way of ascertaining whether a predetermined course of action had the gods' blessings.

In Brooklyn, the tradition of raising and racing homing pigeons, whose innate navigation systems allow them to wing their way home over hundreds of miles, peaked in the late nineteenth century and has since declined. People for the Ethical Treatment for Animals (PETA) considers it cruel, accusing the hobbyists of using the birds' devotional instincts against them, forcing them to endure arduous flights in order to return to their folds. However, witnessing a flock of homing pigeons in flight, underwings pinking in the sun as they arc against the backdrop of a late September sky, their shadows cast, flickering, on the borough's unforgiving surfaces of brick, asphalt, and concrete is, for me, still selfishly a thing to celebrate, a moment to feel very fortunate indeed.

Naively, I have often wondered where birds go to die: so many in the sky, the trees, the power lines, yet rarely seen lifeless, on the ground or anywhere else. Nevertheless, around the time my father was diagnosed with a brain tumor, in July 2003, I observed not only the Rose of Sharon's arrival but also something I could only take to augur ill. I did not just see a dead bird. I saw a bird die.

Behind my townhouse, in that small backyard, the bird, beak parted, flopped back and forth on its side. Had one of the multitudes of mulberries that litter my deck each June lodged in the bird's windpipe? It was excruciating to watch, but there was nothing I could do, so I went inside.

BUT BIRD

Some things you should forget,
But Bird was something to believe in.
Autumn 1954, twenty, drafted,
Stationed near New York, en route
To the atomic tests in Nevada.
I taught myself to take
A train to Pennsylvania Station,
Walk up Seventh to 52nd Street,
Looking for music and legends.
One night I found the one
I wanted. Bird.

Five months later no one was brave
When the numbers ran out.
All equal—privates, sergeants,

Lieutenants, majors, colonels—
All down on our knees in the slits
As the voice counted backward
In the darkness turning to light.

—excerpt from poem by Paul Zimmer, reprinted by permission of
The Permission Company, Inc., on behalf of
University of Arkansas Press

———

Twenty-four years after Reactor Number 4 at the Chernobyl Nuclear
Power Plant exploded in what was then the Ukrainian Soviet Socialist
Republic wildfires in the region began emitting radioactive smoke.

"The smoke will spread, and the radioactive traces will spread. The
amount depends upon the force of the wind," said Vladimir Chuprov, head
of Greenpeace Russia's energy program, in a statement on August 10, 2010.

"[half-tractate]," a poem from Brenda Hillman's *Pieces of Air in The Epic*,
drifted to mind, its words swept like ashes into the bottom corner of
a page:

[—as the too-bright coffin handles were
set down: a slight   breeze   where
      arch is delayed—cirrus clouds in
                  Olema trees   above her cheer; passerine
birds strayed . . .   How did wind feel,
brightness betrayed, entering   such social ground?]

—poem by Brenda Hillman, reprinted by permission of
Wesleyan University Press

Russia's emergency minister warned that the fires could release radioactive particles, but its chief sanitary doctor said, "There is no need to sow
panic. Everything is fine."

Derived from *sānus*:
1. sanitary: of or relating to health
2. sanity: soundness or health of mind
3. sanitize: to make more acceptable by removing
   unpleasant features

During one of my father's three stays at New York City's Memorial
Hospital for Cancer and Allied Diseases (better known as Memorial
Sloan-Kettering and, colloquially, Sloan-Kettering), he announced, apropos
of nothing, "I'm not trying to be Erin Brockovich, but did you know that
my closest neighbor also has a brain tumor?"

We had chosen Sloan-Kettering for its reputation and proximity to
my Brooklyn home, though nearly two hundred miles from his own, a
modest but charming A-frame fringed by birch and pine in Charlemont,
a town of about 1,300 residents in the Berkshire foothills of northwestern
Massachusetts. Sited on a five-acre plot of mostly uncleared land, a
river, the Chickley, hemmed its western border, lending an effervescent
undertow to the soundscape of crows and jays, train whistles, and hounds.

Nathaniel Hawthorne wrote of the area in 1838:

> I have never driven through such romantic scenery, where there was
> such variety and boldness of mountain shapes as this; and though
> it was a broad sunny day, the mountains diversified the view with
> sunshine and shadow, and glory and gloom.

—*Passages from the American Notebooks*, Volume 1

PLOT

Twenty acres of evergreen-thick land, a river
saddle-stitching the west border. The Chickley—
the mighty Chickley—you baptize it. Why not?

10

It is yours now, as much as water can be claimed,
held in the hand. In the Berkshires' grassy foothills,
you keep the walls glassy for the view. Two-

by-fours and forty-two buckets of sweat
equity. All your savings. You pick black granite
from a local quarry for the kitchen counters,

and oh, how that rock sparks in the angling sun!
Drinking water would come from a well—
town lines don't go out this far—but that's swell,

you think. More pure, somehow. And yes,
a nuke plant one mile upstream,
but not to worry—it is being decommissioned.

—poem by the author, reprinted by permission of
Negative Capability Press

———

In 1954, Yankee Rowe Atomic—or Yankee Rowe, as we called it after
the town where it was situated—was designed, constructed, and operated
as a prototype nuclear power plant as part of President Eisenhower's
Atoms for Peace Program. This program's double-pronged promise hinged
on the newly formed International Atomic Energy Agency's (IAEA)
management of a uranium bank. The stockpiles designated for nuclear
weapons would ostensibly supply the uranium for nuclear energy, thus
reducing the threat of atomic war while producing an abundant supply of
juice. Some believed this justification to be propaganda, a covert way for
the US to continue to accrue bomb-making plutonium.

Completed in 1960, Yankee Rowe became the first pressurized water
reactor (PWR)—as opposed to light water and boiling water types—
built in New England and the third in the United States. The prototype,
commercialized in 1961, was scheduled to be in commission for only six
years, but continued to operate for nearly thirty-two. When it closed, on

October 1, 1991, it also became the first PWR, which by then represented the majority of Western nuclear reactors, to be decommissioned. M. S. Terrell and D. McGee of Duke Engineering and Services, say:

> The experiences and lessons learned in the decommissioning of Yankee Rowe span almost every aspect of decommissioning. Many of the current regulations and decommissioning techniques used at plants throughout the United States were developed based upon the lessons learned at Yankee Rowe.
>
> —"Decommissioning Lessons Learned at Yankee Rowe" (March 2001)

If you had visited Yankee Rowe's official website sometime prior to 2013, you would have learned that the plant: **"Began commercial operation in 1961 and was permanently shut down in 1992** *when the plant was determined to be no longer economically viable."* The emphasis, since removed, was theirs—the boldface and italics seemingly designed to be *in* one's face, a middle finger raised counter to the safety concerns of activists, environmentalist groups, and locals who had been calling for the aging plant's shutdown for years.

Why might Rowe's stewards feel the need to wax so emphatic about the reason their facility closed? According to John Mullin, Professor of Urban Planning at the University of Massachusetts, Amherst, and Zenia Kotval, Director, Urban Collaborators and Urban Planning Partnerships at Michigan State University:

> . . . Communities where nuclear power plants close face the same kinds of issues as do those that lose military bases, mental hospitals, or tuberculosis hospitals. They are left with buildings and grounds that usually are aged, difficult to revitalize, failing to meet current standards for production layouts, and poorly located. In one way, however, the problems of reusing nuclear sites are uniquely difficult, for along with the aforementioned obstacles, a seemingly ineradicable stigma is attached to them. . . . Is the stigma magnified because the facility was forced to close, raising the possibility of the closing signifying the failure of a plant that was suspect to begin with?
>
> —"The Closing of the Yankee Rowe Nuclear Power Plant:
> The Impact on a New England Community" (1997)

STIGMA (noun) definition of:
1. a scar left by a hot iron
2. a mark of shame or discredit
3. an identifying mark or characteristic; *specifically*: a diagnostic
   sign of a disease

—

In February 1997, under pressure from local watchdog group Citizens Awareness Network (CAN), the Massachusetts Department of Public Health (MDPH) conducted a health study of the area where my father lived. Referred to locally as the Hilltowns, this cluster of approximately one dozen small, economically-depressed communities was chosen due to its location downriver from Yankee Rowe Atomic, one which represented the greatest opportunity for exposure to the plant's air emissions. Despite an array of disclaimers, the study—*Assessment of Cancer Incidence and Down Syndrome Prevalence in the Deerfield River Valley, Massachusetts*—nevertheless found statistically significant elevations in breast cancer, Down Syndrome, and non-Hodgkin lymphoma, the type of cancer my father had.

My father's diagnosis, specifically, was diffuse, large B-cell type lymphoma (DLBCL), or, more specifically, primary central nervous system lymphoma (PCNSL), a subtype of DLBCL that affects only the brain. Until recently, PCNSL was a rare type of brain cancer that primarily afflicted people with impaired immune systems, and concurrent with the AIDS epidemic, disproportionately affected the gay community.

My father, as it happens, was gay. He came out in the late seventies, when I was seventeen. He came out to my mother, that is, not to me, prior to ending their twenty-year marriage. I discovered his sexual orientation while raiding my mother's sock drawer, finding a letter he'd written to her tucked under a package of No nonsense peds.

Back when peds were better known as a popular form of women's hosiery—slight nylon sheaths that discreetly protected a woman's foot from her shoe leather—and not an acronym for performance-enhancing drugs, homosexuality was simply not spoken of, at least not in my household nor—at least that I'd heard—in the small town where we lived.

Athol, Massachusetts was nicknamed "Tool Town" for its two factories, L.S. Starrett and Union Twist Drill, later known as Union-Butterfield. Small town though it was, the factories were such prominent industrial forces that, twenty-six years ago, upon learning where I was from, my future husband produced an L.S. Starrett micrometer caliper from his Morristown, New Jersey, toolbox as proof of our destiny.

———

SUN-FAINT SUGGESTION

after a painting by Ida Waslaske, c. 1970

Nowhere, Massachusetts—snowdrifts clasp a clapboard white house.
Umbrella trees let loose their leaves, make nestless my house:

a saltbox-shaped egg, a brooding white hen. Multi-paned
windows survey a hillbilly estate—the icy house's

roof creaks under its freight. Come summer, daubs of skunkgrass,
snapdragon, bittersweet. Across the street, a wild house-

less plot where waterfalls skim over slick, mossy rocks.
I cast pine-needle spells, spy red-tailed fox. Sly house

severing once-Civil brothers, a brothel, a moonshine saloon—
A stone cellar scumbled all their secrets in its sides. O, house

was it always roughed out that you'd fumble our lives, too—
blur the bluffs, scar the blacktops that cars died on, house,

guzzling their way home to you? A tractor rusted
in a pit where we'd play witch 'til: *Back inside the house!*

When Dad left, I traced the scent of his shirts, sniffed
out a letter he'd cursed, sighed, and housed

in Mom's sock drawer, confessing he loved men, though
she'd always be his first love. I put up no big fight, house,

when she put you up for sale. You're ice-locked in this painting
Dad traded for a stuffed owl he'd found molting high in the house—

attic where my lissome self unearthed hills of blue hula hoops
flecked with paper flowers. The sun shone at least once on my house.

—poem by the author, reprinted by permission of
Negative Capability Press

———

The ghazal form is ancient, with roots in seventh-century Arabia.
Derived from the nostalgic *nasib* (opening) of the longer Arabian *qasida*
(intention), in which the poet reflects on things passed, the slimmed-down
architecture of the ghazal manages to condense a remarkable amount of
energy around its central concerns of love and loss. The second line of
each couplet, and both lines of the first, conclude with a *qafia* (rhyme)
immediately preceding a *radiif* (refrain). The last couplet is reserved for
a "signature," in which the poet invokes his or her name in some way,
typically in first, second, or third person.

The ghazal was conceived around the same period of time as the first
pandemic of plague. When the events of "Sun-Faint Suggestion" took
place, there was another illness plaguing us: AIDS. Initially thought to
be a gay disease, it was only after American icon Rock Hudson died from
AIDS-related complications in 1985 that it became destigmatized in the
public's perception, as celebrity friends rallied for its medical research in
Hudson's support.

Around then, my father elected to be tested for the HIV virus, too.
The results were negative. Nevertheless, his Sloan-Kettering doctors in
2003 tested him twice more, seemingly determined to find a connection
between his sexual orientation and his cancer. Each round resulted in
the same outcome. When we asked about other risk factors, his doctors

acknowledged three other conditions in which people are known to develop brain tumors: genetics, trauma, and the environment.

In my father's case, there was no genetic history, nor could we recall any significant trauma. However, multiple reputable sources—the American Cancer Society, for one—cite ionizing radiation as an established environmental risk factor for brain tumors. Radiation of the sort that has sufficient energy to interact with matter. Matter, for example, like the human body. Radiation of the sort that is produced in large quantities by nuclear power plants as a byproduct of operation.

———

"What are you working on?" a faculty member at Stonecoast, the University of Southern Maine's low-residency MFA program, asked me in the summer of 2010. I started to offer up some learned response concerning voice and authenticity. Then something broke loose inside: "I'm working on becoming unnumb," I heard someone, who could not possibly have been me, say, as I struggled to stanch my tears.

> MELTDOWN (noun) description of:
> 1. the accidental melting of the core of a nuclear reactor
> 2. a rapid or disastrous decline or collapse
> 3. a breakdown of self-control

The word "meltdown" is not officially defined by the IAEA nor by the US Nuclear Regulatory Commission (NRC). My meltdown officially began midway through an MFA residency that had felt more like poetry boot camp, the first days occupied with an instructor who favored a technique he called "The Interrogation Method." Writing prompts included such questions as: *What have you done with your hands? What have you crossed out? What are the smells that make you think of going back?*

———

One August afternoon in the early '90s, in an attempt to make a pool of water deep enough to swim in, my sisters, our husbands, and I dammed a small section of the Chickley. For hours, we shucked large boulders from the riverbed, reintroducing them one by one into a rudimentary retaining wall.

We had assumed that my father—a man over six feet tall who claimed that his hair, after being rinsed in the river, was as soft as a baby's, but who lamented his inability to immerse himself entirely in "the drink"—would be grateful to us for creating a semi-respectable swimming hole. However, when we proudly announced to him that we had dammed "the mighty Chickley," he chastised us, fake-patiently explaining that damming had all kinds of undesirable ecological consequences.

Back in my Stonecoast poetry workshop, I attempted to explain my meltdown. The words, when I managed to find them, sounded as ludicrous as I had feared: "My father died from a brain tumor that he got from a nuclear power plant." Or something like that—the memory so embarrassing I have almost successfully blocked it.

Seven years had elapsed before I was able to undam this simple, inelegant phrase. I had danced around it, privately, in every possible way, fearing labels like "alarmist," "tree-hugger," "radical." Moreover, while I had written several poems about Yankee Rowe's history and several about my father's disease, I had yet to write the poem that connected the dots, one that indicted Yankee Rowe as the scene of the crime.

It was terrifying to say aloud. Even more alarming was that, once I had admitted my suspicion to myself, I felt a responsibility to warn others, even though, like my father, I had little interest in being Brockovich. An introvert, I could barely bring myself to read my poems aloud in the privacy of my own bedroom, let alone conceive of taking on nuclear power.

———

POWER (noun, often attributive) definition of:
1. ability to act or produce an effect
2. possession of control, authority, or influence over others
3. a source or means of supplying energy; *especially* ELECTRICITY
4. *plural*: an order of angels

Rad. Radical. Radiation. When we look at a word's etymology, we look to its root. In this case, the root, derived from the Latin *radix,* literally means "root." RAD, as an acronym, stands for "Radiation Absorbed Dose," a largely obsolete term for the measure of therapeutic radiation causing one hundred ergs of energy to be absorbed by one gram of matter, resulting in the destruction of malignant cells.

In botany, the radicle is the first part of a plant embryo to emerge from the seed, reaching downward in the soil:

> It is hardly an exaggeration to say that the tip of the radicle thus endowed . . . acts like the brain of one of the lower animals; the brain being situated within the anterior end of the body, receiving impressions from the sense-organs, and directing the several movements.

> —Charles Darwin, *The Power of Movement in Plants* (1880)

In contemporary slang originating with the early 1980's Valley Girls of Southern California, "rad" took on yet another meaning: *Extraordinary. Life-changing.*

ATOMIC ACRONYMS

ASW	Auxiliary Service Water
EP	Emergency Preparedness
ICM	Interim Compensatory Measures
LTP	License Termination Plan
NCV	Non-Cited Violation
NPDES	National Pollutant Discharge Elimination System
ODCM	Offsite Dose Calculations Manual
PDR	Public Document Room
QSR	Quality Surveillance Reports
RCA	Radiological Controlled Area
TI	Temporary Instruction

INCIDENTS & ACCIDENTS

15.01.1991 A lightning strike resulted in fire in a transformer. Loss
of offsite-power, loss of vital buses, and loss of communication . . . - >
scram.

—Antonia Wenisch, "Yankee Rowe in USA,"
No Nukes Inforesource (March 2004)

———

The Chickley River is a major tributary to the Deerfield River, itself
the second longest tributary to the Connecticut River. The Deerfield
drains seventy-three miles from southern Vermont through northwestern
Massachusetts. My husband, Chris, and I often cooled off from the valley's
humid summer days by wading, floating, and generally splashing around
in the Chickley. When we felt ambitious, we would wade down to where
the two bodies of water merged, attempt to swim across the Deerfield, and
inevitably fail. Settling for a sport we referred to tongue-in-cheek as "pole
dancing," we would plant our walking sticks deeply in the riverbed and,
holding tightly to their tops, allow the swift water to lift our legs and float
our feet behind. We would bob there, our bodies tumbling in the froth and
rush—weightless—all our senses alive.

The best time to practice pole dancing was after one of two scheduled
dam releases each day, with the river at its peak. The latter release was
preferable since, by then, the air trapped between the mountains had
become oppressive.

When we thought about it, which was not often, we told ourselves there
was no cause for concern. That Yankee Rowe had been in the process of being
decommissioned for years—that it no longer produced power nor dumped
waste into the river. The Deerfield looked vital. People white-water rafted on
this river, swam and fished in it, grew corn and grazed cattle on its sides.

Yankee Rowe, we assured each other, was going away. On their website's homepage, you might still find a time-lapse animation of the site being deconstructed, piece by piece disappearing, nothing left in its place but level green.

———

Level Green (1990) and *Reactor* (2004) are two of Judith Vollmer's four poetry collections. The former takes the Pennsylvania village of her childhood as its namesake. The latter book's title is, at least in part, a reference to the fact that Vollmer's father, Regis, an artisan machine toolmaker—along with his younger brother and son—all made their careers in the nuclear power industry. All, in fact, had worked at Yankee Rowe or elsewhere in Refuel and Repair, which Vollmer says meant "they went to fix things, and to remove contaminated fuel rods." Descending from a family that, historically, suffered more from heart attacks and strokes than from cancer, Vollmer's father, like mine, was diagnosed with non-Hodgkin lymphoma at the age of sixty-six.

Yankee Rowe rears its bald dome at several points throughout her collection, including the following excerpt from the opening poem:

YUCCA MOUNTAIN SEQUENCE

    i. The Reactor

The dome of heaven was built in a single frame.

                     —Marina Tsvetaeva

I didn't care for my brothers' toys,
even the silver cities that rose under the piano
were part of another stage. I wanted the gray tower
fitted from five hundred pieces, the model someone
designed for whom, unclear; my brothers
placed it, finished, on the gameroom table,

and rejoined their camp in the woods. Someone must
know the code to its tiny red door; someone walked
its halls and polished the white floors,
the Deerfield River ran beside it,
we saw a movie on summer vacation.
Pipes big as tunnels shined plain satin steel. Something flowed
out of the tower and into the cold river
and over the bright scales of fish.
Tower with slippery sides,
dome without windows.

—excerpt from poem by Judith Vollmer,
reprinted by permission of The University of Wisconsin Press

Citizens swim, fish and boat in the river. Wells and cropland are
adjacent to the river, and in times of drought, river water is used to
irrigate crops.

—Deb Katz, *The Carcinogenic, Mutagenic, Teratogenic and
Transmutational Effects of Tritium* (April 1994)

Many of us grow our own food and are in direct contact with the
land. Yankee's plan did not take into account the way we live in
Franklin County. We are a poor rural community.

—Nina Newington, Yankee Rowe Community
Advisory Board member (March 1998)

Poor people are more likely to develop brain tumors but it is unclear
why, researchers reported Tuesday . . . Additional, larger studies may
help shed some light.

—Reuters (May 2004)

My father's brain tumor was not a solid, well-defined mass. Instead, it was deemed "densely infiltrative," the cancer taking the form of numerous tendrils woven through healthy brain tissue—spreading, subdividing, and building an invasive network much like the roots of a weed. Surgery, then, was not an option. Therapeutic radiation was discussed but considered a last resort: It would destroy too much good tissue along with the bad.

Instead, his treatment was to consist of two rounds of chemotherapy, although chemo was problematic, too, due to something called the blood–brain barrier, a protective layer of cells that is difficult for medication to penetrate. However, by exploiting some weaknesses that occur at tumor locations, this barrier tends to become "leaky," making some penetration possible.

Keith Harmon Snow:

> As early as 1966, the six-year-old Yankee reactor faced regular contamination leaks as high pressures and temperatures blew holes in reactor pipes, seals and bearings. Testifying to the technological problem-solving, leaks were found by wrapping tubes with Saran Wrap.

> —"Nuclear Poisons,"
> *Valley Advocate Newspapers* (July 1995)

LEAK (noun) description of:
1. a crack or hole that usually by mistake admits or lets escape
2. *sometimes vulgar*: an act of urinating

SHORT-TERM MEMORY LOSS: CONVERSATION #48

As usual, your face grows thoughtful, then increasingly anxious. You begin picking your fingernails. Because I'm trying to read a book, you clear your throat before you say, *I think I'm going to need to take a leak soon.* I smile and nod, pat your hand. Remind you that you're hooked up to a catheter. *Oh,* you say, as if this were a first. Or sometimes you say, *what's that?* And I explain again that your pee travels down a tube attached to your penis. *Oh,* you say, looking a little offended. *Where does it go?* I point, not wanting to pick it up. *Oh,* you say, *okay,* or sometimes, *yuck.*

The silence lasts about a minute. Then your face grows thoughtful. You begin stealing glances at the bathroom. You clear your throat and I raise my eyes from the book—the page I can't move on from, the sentence I keep having to start—over and over again.

—poem by the author, reprinted by permission of
Negative Capability Press

The substance plutonium becomes interesting to us when we read that certain parts of the building where it is manufactured have leaks. We don't know really what this means. . . . But we know the word "leak" indicates error and we know that there is no room for error in the handling of this substance. All that we know in the business of living eludes us in this instant. None of our language helps us.

—Susan Griffin, excerpt from
Woman and Nature: The Roaring Inside Her (1979),
reprinted by permission of Counterpoint

LEAK (verb) description of:
1. to become known despite efforts at concealment

23

Keith Harmon Snow:

> In Greenfield [Community College], I took a random sampling of
> Yankee documents. Here's some of what I found: . . . Reports 15 to 65
> from February 1962 to May 1966 are missing.
>
> —"Nuclear Poisons," *Valley Advocate Newspapers* (July 1995)

"The disasters numb within us," tolls the opening line of "Life at War"
(1968), Denise Levertov's signature Vietnam War–era poem. Yet the
threat of ultimate disaster in the age of nuclearism, a political philosophy
advocating nuclear weapons and power as keys to national security,
began some twenty years earlier in the Second World War. John Gery's
pioneering work *Nuclear Annihilation and Contemporary American Poetry:
Ways of Nothingness* (1996) posits that since then we—poets included—
have collectively adapted by becoming numb. Annihilation is too much for
us to contemplate. It stunts the limits of our imaginations—we shut down.

His book explores the central task confronting poets writing in the
nuclear age: how to manage the specter of catastrophe that constantly
hovers between pen and page. Gery groups poems written in the nuclear
canon into four categories: 1) the protest poem, 2) the apocalyptic lyric,
3) psychohistorical poetry, and 4) poems of "destinerrance," a term coined
by philosopher Jacques Derrida connoting an amorphous state of being.
Another way of thinking about these divisions, Gery says, is to view them
as poems that speak *against, through, around,* and *from within* nuclearism.

Praising her "radical calm," Gery nominates Levertov as a prime example
of his first category, the protest poet. In the decades following the Vietnam
War, Levertov went on to be an arduous advocate for a host of sociopolit-
ical issues, engaging consistently and prolifically in an interrogation with
nuclearism. In poem after poem, she made it her business to call things out,
to name things, seeming to intuit that the need for a name, like the need
for touch, was basic and spiritual. Her "Mass for the Day of Saint Thomas
Didymus," which follows the six-part format of the liturgy of Mass, praises

many things by name, not least of which names themselves for their ability "to give / to the Vast Loneliness / a hearth, a locus."

One of her early inspirations, Rilke also believed that things so cry out to be named that they don't really exist until we have named them:

> As Rilke describes it in the Ninth Elegy, the redemption of language (which is to say, the redemption of the world through its interiorization in consciousness) is a long, infinitely arduous task. Human beings are so "fallen" that they must start simply, with the simplest linguistic act: the naming of things.
>
> —Susan Sontag, "The Aesthetics of Silence," *Styles of Radical Will* (2002)

Rebecca Solnit asserts a feminist view in *Savage Dreams*: *A Journey into the Landscape Wars of the American West* (1999), her account of atomic bomb development and testing:

> Nowhere is naming as a form of sexual possession more evident than in the West. . . . The land was virgin, untouched, undiscovered, unspoiled, and its discoverer penetrated the wilderness, conquered it, set his mark upon it, claimed it, took possession of it with the planting of his flag or with the plough that broke the plains.

Kim Noriega's first book of poems, *Name Me* (2010), maintains a binary stance, introducing its title with a passage from Barbara Dubois's *Passionate Scholarship: Notes on Values, Knowing, and Method in Feminist Social Science* (1983). The citation's context refers to the lack of vocabulary for domestic violent crimes as well as their victims' understandable reticence to self identify as such and/or report the offenders:

> The power of naming is two-fold: naming defines the quality and value of that which is named—and it also denies reality and value to that which is never named, never uttered. That which has no name is rendered mute and invisible: powerless to claim its own existence . . . this has been the situation of women in our world.
>
> —Barbara Dubois, as cited in Leonard (2002)

The eco-feminism movement, often credited to have been inspired by Susan Griffin's *Woman and Nature, The Roaring Inside Her*, a staple of women's studies curricula, is based on the belief that the social mentality oppressing and doing violence to women is analogous to the social mentality leading to abuse of the environment. Chris Crittenden, poet and professor of environmental ethics at the University of Maine, Machias, explained their ideology to me:

> Although language is potentially versatile, the ritualized ways we use it reflect thousands of years of expansion through violence. History has embedded classification and objectification in the byways of our thoughts, anchored to the superiority of the warrior male, who is defined by an ability to kill with prowess while showing no emotional vulnerability. All of us unconsciously replicate this program and must overcome it in the struggle to reclaim our words, enlisting them to sculpt a mature ethos.

"Deep ecology," a phrase devised by Norwegian philosopher Arnie Naess in 1972, envisions radical changes in humanity's relationship to nature. Instead of focusing on the world as anthropocentric—a resource to be exploited rather than an asset to be treasured—deep ecologists say that an *eco*centric consciousness is more aligned with the reality of the cosmos, that trees, animals, water, and plants are just as necessary, if not more so, to the well-being of this planet as are people.

Many deep ecologists would also self-identify as eco-feminists. However, this is not always a two-way street. Some eco-feminists don't consider themselves deep ecologists because they believe that the real issue at hand is not anthropocentrism, but *andro*centrism or man-centeredness. Yet a third strain, the social ecologists, assert that the environmental crisis directly links to authoritarianism and hierarchy in all forms—not just patriarchy, but also racism, Third World exploitation, and maltreatment of other marginalized groups.

Informally known as the "Poet Laureate of Deep Ecology," Gary Snyder ended his 1969 Pulitzer Prize–winning book of poems *Turtle Island* with "Four Changes," an essay written "in response to an evident need for a few practical and visionary suggestions":

> Whatever happens, we must not go into a plutonium-based economy. . . . —a path once entered, hard to turn back.

———

My father's first chemotherapy treatment was declared a success: His tumor shrank to half its initial size. Unfortunately, it almost took his kidneys along with it. He remained in the hospital for four weeks waiting for his white blood cell counts to return to a standard normally reached in a few days.

The hospital finally released him in September 2003, two weeks after the US Northeast blackout, a surreal ending to his prolonged stay. With Manhattan's traffic lights darkened, and its subway system brought to a halt, the city was impossible to negotiate, and I found myself unable to make it from the Lower West Side where I worked to the Upper East, where my father was lying in a hospital reliant on back-up generators for power.

> The blackout occurred at a time when the Blaster computer worm was squirming its way across the Internet. The timing triggered some speculation that the virus may have played a role in the outage . . . two systems at a nuclear power plant operated by FirstEnergy had been impacted by the Slammer worm earlier in the year.
>
> —Kevin Poulsen, *SecurityFocus* (February 4 and 11, 2004)

"What this [Fukushima] station suffered was a station blackout," says
Deb Katz of the Citizens Awareness Network . . . "and the backup
safety systems that were supposed to keep it operational failed. This
can happen without an earthquake. A Midwest power company
caused the northeast grid to fail a few years ago; a flood or a terrorist
attack could do the same."

—Keith Harmon Snow, "Nuclear Apocalypse In Japan,"
ConsciousBeingAlliance.com (March 2011)

According to my father, September 2003 was a pleasant month in the
Berkshires. Between outpatient treatments at Sloan-Kettering straddled by
overnight stays in my Brooklyn home, we spoke frequently on the phone.
He seemed cognizant again, even hopeful. I'd receive the occasional email:
"We've had two absolutely gorgeous early fall days, sunshine filtering
through the trees and sparkling on the Chickley . . . Oh, yes . . . and guess
what? I can use the computer again . . . and on my own!"

And there was this: "I should tell you that I am less and less resistant
to the idea of full brain radiation." But when it came to radiation
therapy, so-called late or delayed effects were, arguably, as bad as the
symptoms of the tumor itself: forgetfulness and loss of gait, bladder
control, and ultimately, independence.

Because he knew that his tumor affected his short-term memory, my
father relied on Denny and me to advise him. And while he may have
been less resistant to full-brain radiation, we were less than enthusiastic.
We wanted the cancer gone, of course, but not at the expense of his
quality of life, and we believed that, under more lucid conditions, he
would want it that way, too. According to numerous sources, ionizing
radiation in therapeutic doses is the only unambiguous, noninherit-
able factor that has been identified as *causing* certain brain tumors. My
feelings were further complicated by my growing suspicion that radiation

28

absorbed, without his knowledge and certainly not for therapeutic treatment, may have been the origin of his disease.

———

Alle Dinge sind Gift, und nichts ist ohne Gift; allein die dosis machts, daß ein Ding kein Gift sei. (All things are poison and nothing is without poison; only the dose makes a thing not a poison.)

—Theophrastus Bombastus von Hohenheim, popularly known as Paracelsus, "Die dritte Defension wegen des Schreibens der neuen Rezepte," *Septem Defensiones* (1538)

———

The sixteenth-century alchemist Paracelsus, aka The Father of Toxicology, was a revolutionary in his time, concerned with snuffing out unscientifically proven thought and illuminating modern-day thinking about medicine. Not for him the four humors—disease was something that entered the body from *outside*. The abbreviated adage "the dose makes the poison" summed up his belief that any substance—even water, even oxygen—can produce a harmful effect if inhaled, ingested, or absorbed by the body in large enough quantities. This belief built the foundation for current health standards, which specify maximum acceptable-risk concentrations of various contaminants in food, public drinking water, and the environment.

Current ionizing radiation-induced cancer risks are, likewise, based on the linear no-threshold (LNT) dose-response model, which assumes an exact relationship: the higher the dose, the greater the risk. Accordingly, risks at low doses have been extrapolated from high-dose studies; specifically, those studies performed on survivors of the atomic bombings in Japan.

Recent literature, however, suggests that even low, slow doses of some contaminants in water, food, and the environment can result in chronic effects—sometimes even more severe effects than when delivered at fast, high doses. And, in a phenomenon known as the supra-linear effect, other studies have even found that short exposure to low levels of some pollutants or toxins results in adverse reactions, while exposure to high levels has no effect.

Though poorly understood, the idea that low-dose effects may be *different* is fairly well accepted, as evidenced by The Low-Dose Radiation Research Act of 2015, a bipartisan bill passed January 7th by the US House of Representatives, which seeks to clarify the effects of low-dose radiation, motivated in part by concerns about the Fukushima nuclear disaster in Japan.

However, the notion that low doses of radiation might be *beneficial* is more questionable. Proponents point to a phenomenon known as *hormesis*, a term originating from the ancient Greek *hormáein*, "to set in motion, impel, urge on." Hormesis is a generally favorable biological response to a low dose of toxins, or the opposite effect in small doses as in large.

The hormesis model of dose response is divisive among researchers, and generates the most controversy when applied to ionizing radiation. A 2005 report commissioned by the French Academy of Sciences–National Academy of Medicine found sufficient evidence for hormesis occurring at low doses to recommend that it, rather than LNT, be used as the methodology to estimate risks from low-level sources of radiation, such as deep geological repositories for nuclear waste.

—

In December 1992, the MDPH Radiation Control Program collected drinking water samples from six residences located in the towns of Charlemont and Buckland. . . . Results of the analyses showed that all of the samples were below the established regulatory limits. None of the samples detected a positive result for the presence of gamma, gross alpha, or tritium. Three of the samples were positive for gross beta radionuclides. One of these samples detected the presence of gross beta radionuclides above the minimum detection limit of 3 pCi/L, but below the regulatory limits.

—*Assessment of Cancer Incidence and Down Syndrome Prevalence in the Deerfield River Valley, Massachusetts* (Boston, 1997)

—

We believe that Yankee Rowe has been one of the "safest" reactors in the country, according to NRC guidelines. It is the NRC guidelines that need re-evaluation.

—Deb Katz, *The Carcinogenic, Mutagenic, Teratogenic and Transmutational Effects of Tritium* (April 1994)

—

In his essay "Turning Away From the Blast: Forms of Nuclear Protest Poetry" (*War, Literature and the Arts*, 2011), poet Russell Brickey proposes that "All nuclear poetry is protest poetry, as are virtually all movies, novels, and popular music that deal with nuclear bombs, Cold War geopolitics, or nuclear science in general."

Even if not *all* nuclear poetry is protest poetry, it is inarguably the type to which most readers, myself included, have been exposed. Hesitantly, I began drafting poems directly addressing various entities in the Yankee Rowe saga, to the company's board of directors, for example, and to Westinghouse, manufacturer of Yankee Rowe's steam turbine that, on Valentine's Day in 1980, failed "catastrophically," as the industry puts it:

On February 14, a turbine at the Yankee Rowe plant virtually disintegrated. . . . The turbine began to vibrate excessively and came to a stop, badly damaging its discs and blades. . . . NRC officials said that the turbines are outside the reactor containment buildings and are in the non-nuclear parts of the plants. Nevertheless, the commission said, it's possible, though highly unlikely, that a turbine could break and send debris through the containment wall or into cooling pipes.

—*The Argus-Press*, "Nuclear Plant Owners Warned to Check for Cracked Turbines" (May 11, 1980)

Reconciling the strange bedfellows of poetry and polemics can result in artistic catastrophe, too, and the protest poem is where they are just dying to hook up. Even Levertov, the ultimate protest poet, in her 1981 essay

"On the Edge of Darkness: What is Political Poetry?" wondered whether "polemical content" can make for good poetry. She observed that prior to the advent of the printing press, poetry was an oral, communal experience. People welcomed a poem that concerned itself with politics as a decent way of getting the day's news.

By 1620, though, Francis Bacon could write that typographical printing had "changed the whole face and state of things throughout the world." Consequently, lyric poetry—perhaps the most personal mode—came to be more highly regarded than epic, narrative, dramatic, or satiric poetry, according to Levertov, encouraged by the novel's quickly growing affinity for the topics with which these non-lyric modes were traditionally concerned.

By 1955, poetry's purview in matters of mass communication had all but been absolved, as William Carlos Williams observed:

> It is difficult
> to get the news from poems
> yet men die miserably every day
> for lack
> of what is found there.

—excerpt from "Asphodel, That Greeny Flower," *Journey to Love* (1955)

———

ATOMS FOR PEACE

Three decades after the Three Mile Island nuclear accident halted all new reactor orders, President Barack Obama announced $8 billion in federal loan guarantees to build two new nuclear reactors in Georgia.

Five hours into jury pool, I am burned out
on poetry. What I am thirsty for is news.
Good. News.

MSNBC, guide me through
this inverted world, turned back
180 degrees on its stalk.

Enough of this crazy heat!
*I feel impelled to speak today
in a language that, in a sense, is new.*

I, too, would like a plan for clean,
safe energy. One which generates
jobs, ideally, since I am now six

paychecks behind. One that fills
in the pit of partisanship
with some sensible, recyclable waste.

Voir dire. To see them say. False
etymology. I see the president
say it. His lips, that is, are moving.

But how do I know that he believes,
with every atom, his axiom?
Whether he's seen the burning

bush, the worried wind, the patient
sun? Just one. Who stands light-
rinsed for the cameras with the clarity of a star.

—poem by the author, reprinted by permission of
Negative Capability Press

Levertov concludes her essay with the conviction that "whether these poems are good or not depends on the gifts of the poet, not on the subject matter." Whatever poetic gifts I may have then possessed were being put severely to the test. Possibly seeking emotional distance, I initially chose to write my protests as epistles, aka letters, in an archaic, semi-Elizabethan-era diction—the mask of a spiritual witness from a bygone era. When I shared one with my mentor, she told me that, to her ear, the speaker's voice sounded comical. Not quite the effect I had been going for.

Nevertheless, I wondered if humor—intentional humor, that is—might be a way to trick people into reading political poetry, specifically those poems concerning a nuclear power plant. I was beginning to realize I could use all the help I could get. An aging nuclear power plant is not nearly as "sexy" as a bomb. Ninety-nine percent of the poems I had unearthed in the nuclear canon concerned themselves with the prospect of nuclear war, not nuclear energy. Any factory, nuclear or otherwise, is, at least to the untutored, the very definition of routine, tedium, boredom.

———

ITEMS OPENED, CLOSED, AND DISCUSSED

from NRC Inspection Report No. 50-029/2003-002

Opened

> NONE

Closed

> NONE

Discussed

> NONE

After declaring this item "An Official Agency Record," it **will/will not** be released to the public.

—poem by the author

———

My found poem "Items Opened, Closed, and Discussed," from an NRC Inspection Report issued in December 2004, is on the one hand comical because someone saw fit to give nothingness a formal, agenda-like structure. However, it can also be read on another level: As a poem that bears witness to nothing when *nothing* could be less appropriate. The poem thus serves as a whisper-quiet protest. The quietness of it is frightening—grotesque, even.

I recently participated in a workshop that used Philip Thomson's *The Grotesque* (1972) in its syllabus. *The Grotesque* outlines several functions of that style's aesthetic: playfulness, experimentation, and a comic perspective, to name a few. Thomson says:

> It is likely that the play-urge, the desire to invent and "experiment" for its own sake, is a factor in all artistic creation, but we can expect this factor to be more than usually strong in grotesque art and literature, where the breaking down and restructuring of familiar reality plays such a large part.

———

DAD GETS ATOMIC WINGS

My idea of heaven? A place to hang and eat
good food that is, for the most part, bad for you.
Serves alcohol and a decent happy hour, too.

I don't have to wait long in line. It's a calm
place, ideal for striking up conversation.
The wings are bomb, coming in six

stages of explosion. When I'm feeling sanguine,
I get them mild, medium, or hot.
When masochistic, I order the nuclear,

suicidal, or abusive. Food arrives within minutes:
crispy and conducive to detonating
on my tongue like a drunken Baryshnikov

on vacation. Now I can go atomic
without having to leave my home. Hark—
I hear the bell! My deliverance is at hand.

—poem by the author, reprinted by permission of
Negative Capability Press

———

Since I had already been toying with the idea of using more humor in my poems, the grotesque immediately piqued my curiosity. My poem "Dad Gets His Atomic Wings" derives from experimentation with the grotesque as well as with found poetry, using many phrases that I lifted and tweaked from the official website of the Atomic Wings franchise. While I still feel faintly embarrassed by the poem's cartoonish take on the subject of my father's death, I have to admit the take is unique and succeeds in being unsentimental. According to the writer Annie Dillard, turning a text into a poem doubles that poem's context. "The original meaning remains intact," she writes, "but now it swings between two poles."

In 1948, General Electric sponsored *Adventures Inside the Atom,* a promotional comic aimed at adults that told "the thrilling story of man's greatest adventure into the unknown . . ." The same year, *Popular Science* magazine published the pamphlet "Dagwood Splits the Atom," using middle-class cartoon everyman Dagwood Bumstead, a main character in Chic Young's comic strip *Blondie,* as a mouthpiece "to assist you in understanding the atom."

The next generation was similarly prepped to accept nuclear energy as brilliant and benign. From 1953 to 1963, comic books like *Atomic Mouse, Atomic Rabbit*, and *Atom the Cat* were distributed to children. Walt Disney's 1957 animated film *Our Friend, the Atom,* produced with the cooperation of the US Navy and General Dynamics (builders of the USS Nautilus, the world's first operational nuclear-powered submarine), opened its tale of a fisherman and a nuclear genie in a bottle with the proclamation: "Fiction often has a way of becoming fact."

Jump cut to the '70s: A new wave of alternative comic book began to emerge from the minds and hands of concerned writers and artists aiming to reclaim public perception of nuclear power. Leonard Rifas wrote, drew, and self-published *All-Atomic Comics*, featuring "Greedy Killerwatt," a send-up of Reddy Kilowatt, a utility mascot since 1926. And *Slow Death Comics'* Last Gasp series, published in 1978, communicated their position on nuclear power with the facetious titles "Our Friend Mr. Atom" (Greg Irons), Lights Out!" (Errol McCarthy), and "Close Encounters with a Blurred Mind" (Tim Boxell), among others.

———

Growing up, I wanted to become a veterinarian. I owned cats, turtles, hamsters, and a hermit crab. I took riding lessons and saw myself at the helm of a large-animal farm in Vermont one day, like my hero, James Herriot, pen name of veterinary surgeon James Alfred Wight, author of *All Creatures Great and Small.* When it came time to talk to my guidance counselor about future plans, he listened quietly, nodding at my story of finding an injured baby bird when I was six and, with my father's assistance, pitching a tent in my backyard to set up a "practice." He listened silently to all of it and, when I finished, leaned back in his chair, crossed his arms and legs, and said: "Well, sure. All little girls love horses."

Casually, he went on to dismiss my dream job, citing its difficulty, the years of medical school, and the strong stomach it would take. But it was the phrase "all little girls" that gave me pause. I might have been young, but I instinctively recognized that I was being trivialized.

"Little Boy," the name given the bomb that the United States dropped on Hiroshima, was also intended to minimize its scale—the scale of its horror. Psychiatrist Robert Jay Lifton, who focuses mostly on motivations for war in his and Richard Falk's *Indefensible Weapons: The Political and Psychological Case against Nuclearism* (1991) believes that our instinct is to mitigate our anxiety about nuclearism's dangers by minifying the names we give them:

In calling them "nukes," for instance, we render them small and "cute," something on the order of a household pet. . . . Quite simply, these words provide a way of talking about nuclear weapons without really talking about them.

—Lifton & Falk, as quoted in *Nuclear Annihilation and Contemporary American Poetry*, John Gery (1996)

During a lecture at Poets House in New York City, Michael Heller, a leading scholar of Objectivist poetics, spoke about Charles Reznikoff's *Holocaust* (2007), a collection based on verbatim transcripts of the Nuremberg Trials. Heller stated that Objectivists do not seek to impose a viewpoint on the reader but merely aim to make a record of something.

Muriel Rukeyser's *The Book of the Dead* (2003)—a series of poems portraying the story of the Hawks Nest Tunnel Disaster, a hydroelectric project in West Virginia—also contains several poems set in a courtroom. "Statement: Philippa Allen" transcribes a first-hand witness account of a social worker, and "The Disease" is a deposition of a doctor about employee incidents of silicosis, the disease caused by silicate dust in the mines.

Because the poems in *The Book of the Dead* involve injury and death resulting from an energy company's irresponsibility and negligence, I saw them as a natural precedent to the poems I was writing—or trying to write—about Yankee Rowe. Trying my hand at the Objectivist poetry method, I began lightly editing and lineating source texts culled from the Yankee Rowe archive, plundering inspection and industry reports, newspaper clippings, and minutes from town meetings, piecing them together as evidence.

FACILITY NAME: YANKEE ELECTRIC.
FACILITY DESCRIPTION: POWER PLANT

The facility is a small nuclear power generation station,
the third built in the country and the first in New England.

   Little Boy Blue, come blow your horn.

The facility stopped generation in 1992—
is being decommissioned.

   The sheep's in the meadow, the cow's in the corn.

The facility is served by a single potable supply well (02G).
The original well was abandoned during the decommissioning.

   Where is the boy that looks after the sheep?

Numerous local, state, and federal programs regulate activities
at the facility. Well 02G is approximately 280 feet deep,

   Under the haycock, fast asleep.

set into sound bedrock beneath 246 feet of glacial till.
Parts of the facility include radiological storage.

   Will you wake him? No, not I—

The Department determined the well located at the facility
to have a high vulnerability to contamination.

   For if I do, he'll be sure to cry.

—poem by the author, reprinted by permission of
Negative Capability Press

FACILITY (noun) definition of:
1. ease in performance
2. readiness of compliance
3. something (as a HOSPITAL) that is built, installed, or
   established to serve a particular purpose

———

Keith Harmon Snow:

"Facility" or "plant" is too neat, tidy, sterile. Nuclear "power" suggests
strength and security. Nuclear "energy" sings of sunshine and children
playing, not of what it really is: the harnessing of a nuclear bomb.

—"Nuclear Poisons," Valley Advocate Newspapers (July 1995)

———

PLANT (noun) definition of:
1. a young tree, vine, shrub, or herb planted or suitable for
   planting
2. a factory or workshop for the manufacture of a particular
   product, also: POWER PLANT

———

PLANT (verb) definition of:
1. to put or set in the ground for growth
2. to covertly place for discovery, publication, or
   dissemination
3. to conceal

———

Citizens Awareness Network:

"NRC plans to close all Public Document Rooms in the country by
year's end, stifling democratic participation by communities concerned
with contamination from their nuclear corporate neighbors."

In "Facility Name: Yankee Electric. Facility Description: Power Plant,"
I borrow text from a Massachusetts Department of Environmental
Protection report titled "Source Water Assessment and Protection
Report for Yankee Atomic Electric Company." After reading my poem,
one mentor, Ted Deppe, skillfully observed: "In a collection, it lets the
industry and its watchdogs do the reporting, and the poet is like a good
district attorney, reading the letters of the accused to the courtroom and
then asking: 'Do you recognize this letter?'"

Another mentor, Jeanne Marie Beaumont, suggested that I weave in
lines from a fairy tale or folk song to add lyricism to the industrial-speak.
I settled on "Little Boy Blue" for its pastoral setting, not consciously
realizing its suggestion of the Hiroshima bomb's code name until she
pointed it out to me.

In 1989, the nuclear cartoon reached the masses with the launch of
The Simpsons television series. Homer Simpson, the series' main character,
"works" at the fictional Springfield Nuclear Power Plant, thought to be
based on the Trojan Nuclear Power Plant, closed in 1993 due to defects,
near *Simpsons'* creator Matt Groening's hometown of Portland, Oregon.

At Springfield, the workers are as thick as bricks. They pull pranks
on each other, drink on the job, and endanger the residents and natural
environment of Springfield because safety measures at the plant are
nonexistent and safety reports are always corrupt.

Unlike the employees portrayed in *The Simpsons*, those at Yankee
Rowe Atomic, by all accounts, took pride in their jobs and performed
them with an appropriate degree of seriousness and attention. Yankee
Rowe, in turn, provided a certain standard of living to a community that
was, largely, poor.

UMass professors Mullin and Kotval note:

> The nearest major highway, State Route 2 (the Mohawk Trail), is
> eleven miles south of Rowe. From the Rowe exit, a driver would
> move along a narrow road with sharp turns, through the village of
> Zoar and the town of Charlemont. They are among the poorest
> communities in Massachusetts, and look it: scattered mobile homes,
> rural shacks, untilled farms, and abandoned automobiles can be seen
> from the road. But the town of Rowe presents an entirely different
> landscape. Well paved roads, first-class institutional buildings,
> carefully maintained housing units and municipal signs reflecting
> New England's historic character abound. The civic amenities
> include even the town dump, which is a "landscaped refuse garden."

Due to the number and quality of jobs it created, Rowe's neighboring
communities expressed envy that Rowe was chosen over their own
hometowns to be Yankee's site. Even when the chairperson of the NRC
called Yankee Rowe's potential failure his gravest fear, locals remained
loyal, not hesitating to express their irritation. "I call them radicals," said
one resident cited in a 1991 *The New York Times* article describing Yankee
Rowe's dissenters. "They look like they got their latest clothes out of a
Salvation Army box. They go around with pigtails."

RELEASE

> "People in the community were generally unaware that the river was
> radioactive, although it had been noted that since the reactor opened,
> the river never froze." —Deb Katz

We were told it was clean. It looked clean, smelled clean—
even tasted clean. We bought the watercolor

renderings of idealized blues, fearlessly rafted the rapids.
Poked the contamination into holes, pulled beers,

listened to heavy metal. If our boats floated uncertainly,
at least our lives wrung out tidy and sterile.

But as it cut a gash through downtrodden towns,
we had to admit our poor river did not so much

flow as skulk. Even brilliant days reflected inert
gray. All but the hardiest life forms—

Walleye, Lake Chub, Longnose Sucker—
refused to sign the liability waiver.

Yet in the daily struggle of unbecoming, our clannish
lives barely stir. And for trout anglers, a slug's released

each morning. A sinking sensation follows slipstream:
We drank the river today. We'll drink it again tomorrow.

—poem by the author, reprinted by permission of
Negative Capability Press

——

When I opened my door to my father one night in late October 2003, just prior to a long-anticipated Sloan-Kettering appointment, his appearance was shocking. His hair was matted, his face pallid, and his body frail. He said little and, more troubling, his eyes, normally so expressive, registered little emotion. In one politically incorrect word, he seemed lobotomized. Denny later described a harrowing road trip from Charlemont to Brooklyn, my father repeatedly begging Denny to turn around, at one point opening his passenger door while the car was still in motion, saying that he wanted to die.

Once inside, my father walked only as far as the living room couch. I served him dinner there, observing with chagrin that he had trouble simply steering fork to mouth, much of his dinner dropping into the folds of the sofa. I had made one of his favorites—crab cakes, remembering too late that it was one of the items he ordered regularly from Sloan-Kettering's in-patient menu.

Once he had finished eating—or attempting to eat—on the couch, he fell asleep there, too. That was when Denny advised me that he had recently discovered my father, a man typically fastidious about personal hygiene, absent-mindedly urinating in the corner of their bedroom.

—

CRAB CAKES

There was nothing uncooperative
in how you went about eating them—

those crispy golden-brown coated,
brine-tanged, savory-sweet morsels.

Through the maudlin looking-glass
of short-term memory loss,

you feasted on their fleshy charms
like each bite was a baptism.

I think I'll have the crab cakes!

A glimmer in your eye:

I'm going to get the crab cakes.

A conspiratorial smile:

What say we try the crab cakes?

So I'd fold your ragged claw in mine,
waiting for them to arrive,

on the dinged, stainless steel hospital cart
Umesh pushed in on bald, creaky tires.

The day you ate only one bite of your crab cake,
then heaved a sigh and shrugged—

I knew you would molt before the next full moon,
scuttle your way backwards into primordial mud.

—poem by the author, reprinted by permission of
Negative Capability Press

———

At Sloan-Kettering the next day, my father's doctor was clearly dismayed by my father's all-too obvious decline following the second round of his protocol, an outpatient treatment with temozolomide. She confronted Denny and me accusingly.

"What happened?" she asked.

I was shocked into silence, having assumed that, if anything, *we* should have been the ones asking *her* that question. While it was true that Denny had recently told me that my father's condition was deteriorating, I had not fully grasped just how bad it had become. And if I had? Would I have insisted on Dad's appointment being moved up? Would that request have been accommodated? Would it have made any difference in the end?

———

Like an invisible monster, cancer destroyed its victims while their loved ones and physicians could only stand by helplessly. The promise of a cure for this dreaded disease excited the popular imagination and fueled a public craze over radium. . . . If radium could burn or kill skin, perhaps it could destroy tumors. For deep-seated cancers, therapists used glass needles and goose quills that could be inserted into the tumor. Some physicians and less reputable entrepreneurs tried to cure almost any ailment with radium.

—Marjorie Malley, *Radioactivity: A History of a Mysterious Science* (2011)

"We slapped radium around like cake frosting."

—Pearl Schotte, quoted in Claudia Clark's
Radium Girls: Women and Industrial Health Reform, 1910-1935 (1997)

RECIPE FOR YELLOWCAKE

There are more ways than one to arrive at a good yellowcake! Often overlooked, dense yet light in consistency, after you have practiced making one or two, you will find yellowcake can be made very quickly, particularly if you are one of the fortunate few to own the latest in sophisticated equipment.

1. Preheat the oven to 2878 °C.
2. Crush raw ore to a fine powder by passing through a series of industrial-sized crushers and grinders.
3. Bathe the resulting pulped ore with concentrated acid.
4. Leach out the uranium and, after drying and filtering, set aside.

Be sure to filter well, or your yellowcake may turn out to be a gray cake, depending on the number and type of impurities that remain.

5. Smelt into purified UO_2, taking care not to scorch.
6. To enrich, combine with fluorine, and pass through a gas centrifuge.

Enrichments complete the whole master system of yellowcake-making!

7. Cool.
8. Cool again.
9. Cool some more. Yellowcake must be thoroughly cold before it can be iced.

Storage

Yellowcake may be stored in the desert for hundreds of thousands of years.

—poem by the author, reprinted by permission of
Negative Capability Press

For forty years, radium was the "it" girl element, added to everything from water to butter, toothpaste to tea. Among the more infamous products were luminescent clock and watch faces painted with the radium-laced, poetically named paint *Undark*. The young women painters were trained to "lip-point" their paintbrush's tips, while the plant's chemists used lead screens, masks, and tongs when in proximity with the substance. Many of the women began to suffer anemia, bone fractures, and rotting of the jaw:

> Their hair, faces, hands, arms, necks, the dresses, the underclothes, even the corsets of the dial painters were luminous. One of the girls showed luminous spots on her legs and thighs. The back of another was luminous almost to the waist. . . .
>
> —"Necrosis of the Jaw in Radium Workers,"
> *Journal of Industrial Hygiene* (August 1925)

One plant worker, Grace Frye, decided to sue, and five other workers, later dubbed the Radium Girls, joined her. It took two years to find a lawyer willing to go up against the affluent US Radium Company and the high-powered lawyers it could afford to retain, but when the suit finally moved forward, the widespread publicity surrounding the case effectively launched new legislation overseeing national labor safety standards and workers' rights. The case was settled in the autumn of 1928; each woman awarded ten thousand dollars, an annual annuity of six hundred dollars, and payment of all medical and legal expenses for the rest of their lives.

FATHER RADIUM'S DAUGHTERS

Once, fingertips waggled flowery from closets
where factory girls ghosted to laughter.

After hours tracing minutes over dial faces,
those girls were glow-colored.

Later, gums ulcerated, mandibles detached.
Still, these always ever after girls

could speak no more than doubt. How
could they blaspheme quills

once kissed, remembering unshadowed
eyes, how they drew Jacks

to lanterned smiles. Even unsequined
dresses twirled constellations.

Unearthed: their bones, still
ethereal, shine.

—poem by Brenda Mann Hammack,
used by permission of the author

The apocalyptic lyric poem, Gery's second category of nuclear poetry, engages with the poet's personal feelings of vulnerability about its dangers, working into metaphor the imagery and lexicon of nuclearism now ubiquitous in the American consciousness. He cites Stephen Dunn's "The Cocked Finger," which likens "The finger that might / touch [the bomb] off" to "an apostrophe on the wrong side of a possessive, / an error so obvious/ almost everyone can see it." Adrienne Rich's "Trying to Talk with a Man" relates a malfunctioning romantic relationship to bomb testing, with one partner accusing the other of "talking of the danger /as if it were not ourselves / as if we were testing anything else."

Gery's book finds Richard Wilbur, a poet who served as a cryptographer during World War II, a master of the sub-genre. Wilbur says:

> In each art, the difficulty of the form is a substitution for the difficulty of direct apprehension and expression of the object. The first difficulty may be more or less overcome, but the second is insuperable; thus every poem begins, or ought to, by a perception of the hopelessness of direct combat, and a resort to the warfare of spells, effigies, and prophecies.
>
> —Richard Wilbur, excerpt from *Responses: Prose Pieces 1953-1976*,
> as cited in Gery (1996)

I have yet to find a more apt explanation for the block I was experiencing when trying to write poems expressing my belief that my father's brain cancer was linked to Yankee Rowe. My trepidation came not only from fear of the subject itself but also from hopelessness in how to express it more or less accurately—how to get the science right— though my belief, profound as it was, could never be proven.

———

Dad was readmitted to the hospital in mid-October 2003. They ran more tests, tried to figure out a new treatment. Full-brain radiation was likely the only remaining option.

In his hospital bed, in a thin blue gown, my father called me over to his side. Quietly but clearly he said, "I want to go."

"Where," I said, "to the bathroom?"

"No."

"Where then, home?"

"No."

Finally, it dawned. "You want to *go,* go?"

He nodded, covering his eyes with one hand. I tried to make him feel heard while at the same time reminding him, selfishly, that his tumor was affecting his decision-making, that the brain tumor board was meeting the next day to try and agree on a way to reduce the lesion's size.

He nodded again, turning his face to the wall.

— • —

ANNIVERSARY

I'm ready to go, I told you that night,
then started to take it back—
when I saw the blue of your eyes.
Your butter knife paused mid-air,

startled to be taken back
to the sweetness of challah bread
poised in the air. Your butter knife.
Mulberry wine turned sour.

Crusts of challah and sweetbreads.
Clocks slump. I curse my grief.
I mull berry wine, but it turns, it sours.
How would you like him dressed?

I slump and grieve the curse of clocks
that cannot tell you their reasons.
How would I like him *dressed?*
I confess: In that month of black things,

I could not have told you the season.
I pulled out the suit you were married in
(the month you confessed to black things)
dyed a moon-eclipsed night.

Your suit. The clothes you married in.
A collared white shirt with a tie
the color of lip-swoon, night-dyed.
Ginkgo leaves swirled on a silk swath.

A white-colored shirt with a tie
that undertook not to choke you.
Ginkgo leaves swirl on a silk cloth
in a pine box. October is a hard month.

It takes you under, chokes you,
puts blues in your eyes.
October is a hard mouth. Pined for.
You told me that night: *I'm ready to go.*

—poem by the author, reprinted by permission of
Negative Capability Press

    I can think of no poetic form that holds uncertainty in precarious balance as well as the pantoum. A Malaysian verse composed of a series of quatrains, the second and fourth lines of each stanza are repeated as the first and third lines of the ensuing one, repeating the pattern, sometimes with subtle, sometimes more creative, variations, until the final stanza, where the third line of the first stanza becomes the second, and the first line of the poem also serves as the last. The repetition, like that of the ghazal, suggests obsession and second-guessing—the perfect form to express my lack of confidence in understanding, let alone mastering, the technical material I was attempting—one step forward, two back—to render poetic.

    For when I tried to educate myself about the full continuum of that plant's history—the black holes, the quantum physics, the self-sustaining chain reaction of it all; the Bohrs, the Frisches, the Hahns of it all; the Planck's constant, Manhattan Projects, Uncertainty Principles of it all;

the Curies, the Cold War, the communist and capitalist of it all—my mind, to use a nuclear metaphor, imploded.

"The Testimony of J. Robert Oppenheimer" (1986) by Ai, a poet most famous for her dramatic monologues emanating from the throats of the infamous, is a sort of armchair analysis of its namesake, widely regarded as the "Father of the Atom Bomb." The testimony in this dramatic monologue seems to equate the creation of the bomb to the urge for self-destruction, to champion the notion that embracing our base tendencies is akin to liberation:

> till like the oppressed who in the end
> identifies with the oppressor,
> we accept the worst in ourselves
> and are set free.

The poem is representational, Gery proposes, of what he calls psychohistorical poetry, his third category of poems in the nuclear canon. Rather than focusing on protest politics or personal experience, the psychohistorical poem—which borrows its name from the discipline spearheaded by psychiatrist Robert Jay Falk—holds one eye on key events of the past while the other attempts to envision the future. Psychohistoric poems, then, present a snapshot of the psychic repository of our culture, account for our shared history through the aperture of the subconscious.

"He was a shy, delicate boy . . . who was more concerned with his homework and with poetry and architecture than with mixing with other youngsters."

—"J. Robert Oppenheimer, Atom Bomb Pioneer, Dies,"
The New York Times (February 19, 1967)

The US effort to develop a nuclear weapon came during World War II in response to the threat of German-made nuclear arms. In December 1941, President Roosevelt appointed a committee, and six months later, that committee, led by J. Robert Oppenheimer, recommended a fast-track program code-named the "Manhattan Project" that would cost up to a hundred million dollars and potentially produce the weapon by July 1944.

The Manhattan Project was so named because the New York City borough of Manhattan was home base to at least ten work sites, including a skyscraper headquarters directly across from City Hall. When enough progress had been made, a test of the plutonium implosion device was performed in Alamogordo, New Mexico, to evaluate whether the weapon would work and the extent of its effects. Oppenheimer named the world's first nuclear detonation test "Project Trinity."

———

There is a poem of John Donne, written just before his death, which I know and love . . . : "As West and East / In all flatt Maps—and I am one—are one, / So death doth touch the Resurrection." That still does not make a Trinity, but in another, better known devotional poem Donne opens, "Batter my heart, three person'd God;—."

—J. Robert Oppenheimer, referencing Donne's
"Hymne to God, My God, in My Sicknesse" (c. 1623 or c. 1631) and
"Sonnet XIV" from *Holy Sonnets* (1633)

———

DADDY DEAREST,

Under the crepuscular shadow of your big-brimmed porkpie hat,
size 6 7/8, I was born an ovoid shape, a fractured light.

I would have preferred to have dropped into hands
more self-aware. Your fingers clung to smoke—

your quasar-blue eyes radiated waves of overreaching
intensity. You: a cloud of nebulous material drawn together

by your own gravity. Not content to be mere Coordinator
of Rapid Rupture—but Father, Son, and Holy

Ghost. O, thunder-stealer, if there were a single art form
that captures your magnetism, it would have to be poetry

or perhaps architecture. With their synthesis, you knew sin,
and this is a truth you could never lose, no matter how cold,

potent, or many fine martinis. O, daddy dearest, I am torn
from your own liver, I am you regenerated into liquid

courage-coded desire, the mystery of your never-love
embroidering me like a fog! O, humanist haunted

by the desert-skeletal terrain, one night I overheard you
talking to yourself darkly under lucid blue stars:

It isn't that I don't feel bad, it is that I do not feel worse
tonight than I did last . . .

Papa, let me lull you from your torture. Permit me to
modulate your memory charitably from the mourning

dove's minor key. I released you when you unleashed me—
poured out my permanent shadow in a great flood

to liberate the parent sod, great linguist of eight tongues!
In a serenade, Daddy, one can choose to sing any song she loves.

—poem by the author

On a clear late-October morning, I was at the post office picking up
a care package my older sister had sent for my father when I received a
frenzied phone call from Denny: "He almost stopped breathing. He's been
put on a respirator. It's supposed to be curative."

54

I managed to arrive at the hospital's intensive care unit just in time to view, through a door implausibly left ajar, my father bucking in his bed, fighting to yank the tube out of his throat while personnel in white garb repeatedly pinned him back down. As I watched him thrash, the image of the sparrow that had appeared earlier that summer to be choking on my deck flew to mind.

I went around the corner to speak with Kathy, one of my father's favorite nurses. She greeted me with sad eyes.

"Tell me," I said.

"This is his worst nightmare," she said. She knew my father well by now, knew that his living will stipulated that he did not want life support unless it was expected to be curative.

"But Denny said the doctor told him that this was a temporary, curative measure," I said. "That this wasn't life support."

"Is that what they told him?"

—

My father had pneumonia. Soon, it was time. The doctors signed off on him in a document stating that he would not survive absent the ventilator. Not to mention the feeding tube, the central line, the catheterization—in fact, pretty much all the therapy typically used to sustain a patient's life, Kathy later informed me—absent a pacemaker.

While the pros for initiating mechanical ventilation had clearly been conveyed—and I, too, wanted to hope that it would be curative—I was not so confident that the cons had been given equal billing. Had the doctors informed Denny, for instance, that my father's mouth, teeth, and upper airway could be damaged while the tube was being placed? That, once placed, the tube could injure the vocal cords? And that its presence placed him at increased risk for pneumonia, the ultimate cause of his demise?

When the doctors were finally out of options, our decision to remove the ventilator seemed like the only choice to be made, although, from time to time, I'll hear about someone who recovers after a prolonged period on life support, and curl into myself, cringing, hugging my sides.

———

The NRC estimates that annual exposure to a hundred millirems of radioactivity—which is within acceptable, legal limits—results in approximately one extra additional death per each 286 people exposed. In other words, NRC regulations . . . are actually designed to justify the taking of lives by nuclear corporations. This legalizes the murder of human beings, as long as the total number of premature deaths is acceptable to the government and the nuclear industry.

—Citizens Awareness Network, *The Radioactivist* (2010)

DISPOSAL

Tuesday, a container (40,000 pounds of low-level irradiated material from Yankee Rowe Nuclear Power Station) slipped off a truck bed, spilled contents along a road in Rowe.

A highly radioactive reactor minus its fuel rods made its way from Massachusetts by rail across North Carolina for burial in South Carolina.

In addition to materials with low levels of radiation, trucks carried paints made of PCBs, and materials with asbestos.

Releases from Yankee Rowe's plant and emissions of tritium: attributed to an increase of disease in the Valley.

Inadequate chains are blamed. Yankee Rowe plans to abandon containers that require being chained to truck beds. They will now be secured with special locking pins.

Accompanied by their children, protestors dressed in protection masks drove mock radioactive waste casks around the building. *Death's garbage can,* one protestor called it.

In all, 2,500 shipments are expected.   The floodgates of waste are opening.
Approximately 600   1 in 10,000 will die
completed.   from radioactive exposure
during nuclear waste transportation.

Towns are not notified about   This: The number of deaths from
the truck routes.   shipments allowed by the NRC.

—poem by the author, reprinted by permission of
Negative Capability Press

Half - Life

Half-Life

You know that dusty white film found on clusters of grapes that diffuses their almost unbearably sensuous, hypnotically deep purple? In nature's perfect wisdom, the grape plant produces the substance to protect its berries from losing their juice. The resulting hue—desaturated Concord grape—was the color of my father's favorite bandanna.

It came into my possession still tied into the triangle he had cinched around his head. A year passed before I could bring myself to pry it apart. Printed with white paisley teardrops and charcoal-etched flowers, the bandanna had been lovingly worn and washed until nearly threadbare—the beginning of a frayed hole near the "Crafted with Pride in America" logo.

He mostly wore bandannas to hide bad hair days, and I think he favored purple because it flagged gay pride. Bandannas are fetishy in gay circles; a certain shade of the color loosely brands their tribe. I clearly remember his ode to the bandanna as object. He praised the cloth workhorse as much for its versatility and value—two for a dollar at Avery's General Store—as for its style.

He used them as napkins, handkerchiefs, dust rags, scarves. He would wrap one around his forehead when gardening to keep sweat from his brow, then fashion it into a carryall for cuttings. On his widening bald spot, they worked wonders.

The effect of a bandanna on the head of this 6' 2", 250-pound man—coupled with the small sterling hoop hanging from his left earlobe—was part hippie, part swashbuckler, and when it was the purple bandanna, undeniably and defiantly gay. Somewhat embarrassingly so, as I've never quite gotten over the cringe factor of learning, at age seventeen, that my father favored men. Cringe-factor of faggot, fairy, flamer, fudge-packer. "As sick as they come," in the words of a character coming out in the movie *C.O.G. (Child of God)* upon being asked if he was one of *those sick ones*.

I began to fall in love with one gay man after another. First, the French horn player who brought me close to ending myself when he ended us abruptly and without explanation. His flint-blue eyes, though, suggested everything I instinctively knew.

Next, I fell for the double-bass player who taught me how to steal industrial-sized packages of cheese from the campus cafeteria where we worked. I loved it when he told me I was "the one," the only woman capable of breaking his habit of sleeping exclusively with men. He had plump plum lips and dyed his fauxhawk purple. He slicked Brilliantine through it, called it *aubergine*.

But my father's favorite bandanna was more the color of an eggplant's flower. Oh, let's just call it by its name: lavender. The lavender bandanna was reserved solely for his head and never subjected to any task less dignified than accessorizing. Other colors in his collection were relegated to lowlier places—the neck, the wrist—and humbler tasks—cleaning and nose-blowing. Occasionally, he'd mix it up, wiping down a tabletop with the blue one, say, before throwing it in the wash and wearing it later that day.

In his photography studio, bandannas held what hair he had left out of his eyes, and at openings, he imagined they lent him street cred. He once shot a self-portrait of his butch alter-ego, wearing a black bandanna, a leather biker-patch vest, and a don't-fuck-with-me glare.

I briefly considered, for this story's sake, whether to say he wore bandannas in the hospital when he lost his hair to chemo, but that would not be true. He might have relied on them had he actually gone bald, but then again, he might have embraced his denuded dome with dignity.

For a long time, I kept his bandanna in my bathroom and used it as a makeshift shower cap. It wasn't so much effective as comforting during the frequent showers I took to cry privately. At some point, probably post-shower and before a fitful nap, it found its way to my nightstand and has stayed there ever since. This ensures that, after five years, with the sharpest grief finally behind me, I still think of my father at least once a day.

Before going to sleep, I drape it over my alarm clock's face to diffuse the cool glare of its digital display—yet another use for this versatile square of cloth. But every so often, the light finds that frayed hole and bleeds through it, interrogating my dreams.

GOOSE QUILLS

Goose Quills

My alarm clock bleeps me slowly out of a deep REM sleep. It's Halloween, 2010, and I am, once again, ghosting Sloan-Kettering—this time, as an employee. I was hired in 2005, two years after my father's death, as a web specialist in the public relations department. I told my family and friends I was leaving my seven-year career at Barnes & Noble.com to do something more humanitarian, less commercial. My therapist said it was an urge to return to the scene of the crime.

Nevertheless, I congratulated myself on making the right decision when, on my first day of work, still looking for signs, I noticed a copy of *The Medusa and the Snail* on the bookshelf across from my desk. My father had given me a copy of the book when I was a teen with a budding interest in writing. Perusing it as an adult, I noted for the first time that its author, Lewis Thomas, was president of Sloan-Kettering in 1995.

The book's namesake creatures depend on each other for survival in a strange symbiotic relationship, each at different times devouring the other, reminiscent of the two purported arms of the Atoms for Peace program. Flipping through the pages, my eyes landed on the essay titled "The Hazards of Science":

> The code word for science and scientists these days is "hubris." Once you've said that word, you've said it all; it sums up, in a word, all of today's apprehensions and misgivings . . . Today, it is strong enough to carry the full weight of disapproval for the cast of mind that thought up atomic fusion and fission as ways of first blowing up and later heating cities. . . .
>
> —Lewis Thomas, *The Medusa and the Snail* (1979)

One of my first assignments at Sloan-Kettering was a photo shoot with a key member of my father's medical team, the obvious goal of which was to make her look like a movie star. I remained stoic, reminded myself of the greater good. Nine months of such assignments later, though, I left my new job on short notice, exhausted from keeping a stiff upper lip and citing "too many ghosts."

Then, some two years and three jobs later, I was beginning to wonder if I had been too hasty. I contacted my former Sloan-Kettering boss to inquire if she had any freelance work. As it so happened, she did. She had just been diagnosed with ovarian cancer and needed someone to manage the website's redesign while she fell off the side of a cliff.

Now I do most of my work from home, only visiting the hospital for weekly meetings. There are still ghosts, and sadly, my boss soon joined their ranks, but those ghosts, for whatever reasons, feel somewhat friendlier this time around.

———

At a recent weekly meeting, concerned with obtaining fresh photography for the Sloan-Kettering website, we lamented the lack of patient faces humanizing its pages. Privacy laws aside, patients who will consent to allowing their images to be used online for promotional reasons are rare. Think about it: You have just been diagnosed with cancer—is this really the moment for your close-up? The shot, then, is always from behind, looking over the patient's shoulder at the doctor's hopefully wise and kindly visage.

We discussed reaching out to Comskil for assistance. An acronym for Communication Skills Training Program in Oncology, Comskil is an in-house service offered to doctors by the hospital's Department of Psychiatry and Behavioral Sciences practice. Professional actors coach the physicians in how they can achieve approachable body language and maintain facial expressions that convey empathy and warmth.

Our hope was that the Comskil actors might be willing to pose in photography shoots as patients—something that staff, upon hire, must sign releases agreeing to do, but who do so as convincingly as one might imagine.

A colleague dubbed Comskil "detention for doctors," adding that the doctors do not choose to participate in it but are required to do so as a type of punishment, and are made to pay for it out of their own pockets.

However, in the official description for the program's initiative, the fine print reads: "Invitation to participate in this pilot project does not mean that a problem with communication has been identified in your doctor's practice."

———

Good bedside manners or bad, the doctors at Sloan-Kettering are rock stars—the chosen ones. Their patients, too, are chosen. Not everyone with cancer is able to gain admittance to the hospital. Conditions are vague and complicated.

After we had identified the hospital as one of the top three in the nation for cancer care and considered its location nearby my home, it seemed the logical next step was to have my father admitted there. But when I called to arrange for our first appointment, I felt interrogated. *How did I get this number who had referred me what kind of insurance did I have?*

When I finally accompanied my father to his intake interview, the brain surgeon's assistant said we were sitting there primarily due to sheer determination.

As soon as we entered the place, I felt it: An energy like static electricity charged the air. In the lobby, at the elevator bank, even in the cafeteria, the building exudes a bristling sink-or-swim-no-time-to-eat-must-save-lives vibe. It felt like an alternate universe, and I knew, for better or worse, we had arrived.

The man to whom my father's doctor reported was referred to in reverent tones as The Grandfather of Neurology. The first time he made an appearance at rounds, I had some questions for him—too many, apparently. The next day, my father informed me that Gramps had circled back to have a little chat with him about my being "too vigilant." I also asked too many questions of the doctor in charge of my father's care in his final days in the ICU. Fed up with my interview, probably in part because he could not give me the answers I was hoping for, he asked, point blank, if I was a nurse. He asked this fully knowing the answer. He asked—in the parlance of performance poets—to slam his point home.

VIGILANCE

Once you caught   kept
          a glimpse of me coming, and I, you going
and you were trying
three nurses were trying   thrashing   fighting
every cell of you screaming
no   and that jar of sputum on your nightstand
one-third of the way full—
putting me in the mind of

my head feels too full   my head feels too
and   and there's my daughter, there she is
there— a lava lamp.
That's what your room needs.

Dr. Omura says to watch you closely for:
1. memory
2. concentration
3.

Thankless November. These doctors are rock stars and I am not
a nurse. I repeat: *I am only his*

How much longer? Six months to two years? Two months to six years?
Brain Tumor Board meeting. Wednesday, 9 A.M.
Decision: Double up the steroids.

The lights blink yellow and blue and red and gold, and that painting
is crooked the pillows are slipping down the sheets you will get
bedsores and I can't straighten it's too hard, too heavy beneath—

In the middle of the night, Rose says you wake up.
          Will you—
Will your eyes ever again call me *daughter*?

Dr. Omura says we are at the maximum levels of what the respirator can
blue and if he keeps going the way he is difficult to give him enough slowly
taking a turn oxygen hovering between the last two levels he might not
he might she will discuss this with you further   and further and
further away—

We can help with arrangements.
A special flight?
There are a few things, but probably not
         much   aiming for   make it
 a few good months.

Charlemont. Sun filtering through the pines.
Flickering, then settling, on the pool.

—poem by the author, reprinted by permission of
Negative Capability Press

———

I've recently rediscovered Abba Kovner's *Sloan-Kettering* (2002), a
book that fell into my hands shortly after my father's death, when I was
still working at Barnes & Noble.com. Kovner, I learned, was a leader of the
Lithuanian resistance during World War II and was central, post-war, in
assisting Jews to escape from Eastern Europe.

I do not know how Kovner came to be treated for throat cancer at
Sloan-Kettering, described in the book's introduction as "that great
fortress of hot science and cold sweat" by Leon Wieseltier, *The New
Republic* publisher. What I do know is that this great poet and activist
must have written the following poem around the same period of time he
elected to have his vocal cords removed:

SLOAN-KETTERING

Sloan-Kettering (its full name: Memorial
Sloan-Kettering Cancer Center)
is a large and growing building
and all those who come within its walls

to strip
naked,
jointly and separately,
suddenly find themselves
in a cage, captive, exposed

—excerpt from poem by Abba Kovner,
reprinted by permission of Schocken Books

Someone else who found herself in that great fortress or cage was my friend Lynn Shapiro. An award-winning former dancer and choreographer, Lynn began writing poetry after being diagnosed with breast cancer in 2000. In 2011, at the age of fifty-two, she won a Pushcart Prize for her poem "Sloan Kettering." Several years later, she died from complications of the disease.

I first read Lynn's award-winning poem during a workshop we were both taking at New York City's Poets House. Even then, with her poem in its early stages, still quite fresh and a bit rough around the edges, it was one of the most moving poems I had ever read.

SLOAN-KETTERING

One thing they don't tell you about Sloan-Kettering
is how beautiful the workers are, shepherdesses, sirens,
brawny football players, ready to lift the heaviest bodies. One,
rosy as a mountain child moves like the most even glare of light,
never turns away till you have risen to follow her.
She holds your paper file near her breasts, but not too tight.
Walls are paved with photographs, scenes of mountains, forests
carved by light. The chemotherapy suite is a skylight, a bubble.
You pass posters for support groups presented on easels like paintings
in progress. For each patient, there are private rooms with chairs
and blankets and a straight-backed chair for a companion if you have one
and a little television with its snake arm, riveted into the wall.
In the center of all these private rooms are gatherings of high stalked
        flowers,

magenta, purple, amber, bursting higher than churches, in golden vases
everywhere, and the carpet is gold, too, so padded you can hear
no sound of walking. There are so many workers here,
and your surgeon, Alexandra, is the most beautiful worker of all.
Her office where you wait is the color of cool green and mountain cream.
A computer pulses out deep blue insignias; next to it
is a magazine, half the cover missing, torn, or half-eaten,
waiting for you to touch it in the same place as the person before you.
You don't and this decision—its stillness, its inability to reverse—is
        profound
and stagnant. Outside in the hallway other doctors stand leaning, writing
with the concentration of food-eating animals, whose only purpose
is to become blind to everything but their own sustenance.
And she is the Sun. She is beautiful when she enters, says *How
are you?* You lean on her *are.* She opens your robe like the earth,
and you say, *I used to have beautiful breasts,* and she says, *You still
do,* and she cups your breasts. This is her special way. She cups
each one, then combs down, down with her fingers as if down
the side of a mountain she is scaling tenderly so as not to fall
once. She half-closes your garment and you close the rest.
You watch her fingers leave your robe how they arc in the air
to papers on her desk, and you realize that at various times
in the past five years you have thought of her fingers, their short
nails, and how she called you and said into the mouth of her phone,
really as an afterthought, that *in the site of the malignancy we found
a little milk. A little* she said, like the purr of a cat, and you could see
her fingers, her surgeon's fingers holding her own children's milk bottles,
and then as you will always, you will want to be like her, to save lives
during the day, then go home, feed your children at night.
You remember the way out on the soundless carpet.
Your husband is with you, murmurs, your husband,
the lobby, just as you remember, in subtle shades, tones of green and gold.

          —poem by Lynn Shapiro, reprinted by permission of the author's estate

———

When I shared Lynn's poem with a female colleague in Sloan-Kettering's public relations department—one who had worked there for many years, her response was: "Why is it always the ones with breast cancer who think they are special?"

———

Too easy to condemn them, though, those jaded, unsung heroes of the hospital, not to mention the doctors they are paid to make look like its real heroes, many with God complexes and salaries to match. The things they must see, must do. After numbing their patients with painkillers and anesthesia, what else but to anesthetize themselves emotionally, too?

> The awful reality of the practice of medicine is that physicians could not function adequately if they were unable to turn off their emotional reactions and distance themselves from the pain . . . they are expected to simultaneously feel and not feel.
>
> —Susan L. Bloom, MD,
> "Emotional Anesthesia: The Double Bind for Doctors,"
> *The Psychotherapy Review* (1999)

At the end of my day as a web developer, I can obtain instant gratification by looking at what I have built out of seemingly thin air: out of pixels, ones and zeroes, bits and bytes. From nothing—something. The same could be said for writing. On a good day, at least.

But at the end of their days, how often could my father's doctors pat themselves on their collective backs? Their job, at least in my father's case, was less about building, more about decommissioning. And, as evidenced by Yankee Rowe's experiments, sometimes it's easier to create than to destroy.

———

> The process (of dismantling a nuclear power plant) is called decommissioning and is like no other deconstruction or dismantling effort. Some of the specific tasks that must be performed . . . have never been done before and are only going to be done once. Each

part of a nuclear power plant is meticulously analyzed, removed and discarded according to strict waste classification criteria. The reason: There's no margin for error.

—*Civil Engineering Magazine* (April 2001)

————

"Bigger," my father's doctor said, when I inquired how the tumor looked after the second round of chemo.

"How much bigger?" I wanted to know, evidently again too vigilant or, at least, more inquisitive than the physician cared to entertain.

"Bigger," she repeated, this time with a bite.

————

brain tumor—

a bear breaking through

the skylight

————

After my father died, the same doctor sent me a condolence letter. It is brief, but not cold, written on a lithographed sheet of quality vellum picturing bare, November trees:

> Dear Denny and Lissa,
>
> I was so sorry to hear that Dennis died last week. You all did a wonderful job taking care of him. I have enclosed a favorite poem of mine that always provides some comfort when I lose someone dear to me. Take good care of each other.

My father's doctor had no inkling of my interest in poetry. I imagine she keeps copies of that poem on hand to supplement her sympathies, like a pharmacist in Boston I have heard about who dispenses a poem with each prescription. However, the fact that a scientist turned to poetry at the most difficult moment of all speaks to poetry's power to span pronounced distances between disparate parties. In "The Rare Union: Poetry and Science" from *The Life of Poetry* (1996), Muriel Rukeyser writes:

> If there were no poetry on any day in the world, poetry would be invented that day. For there would be an intolerable hunger. And from that need, . . . poetry would be—I cannot here say invented or discovered—poetry would be derived.

By now, I had tried my hand at three of John Gery's four schools of nuclear poetry: the protest poem, the apocalyptic lyric, and the psychohistoric. Though significant intersections could be observed between them, I could see and hear the ruptures in their aesthetics and concerns. However, when I tried to grasp the finer distinctions of his last classification of nuclear poems, the so-called "poems of destinerrance," I floundered. I was unable to find the Derrida-coined term in my dictionary.

Googling the word revealed that it connoted a state of being that falls between the cracks: one that exists somewhere between destiny, inheritance, and errancy. Gery praises the work of John Ashbery as the touchstone for his last category, particularly Ashbery's earliest work, which, he points out, seems more interested in exploration than explanation. In Ashbery's "The Absence of a Noble Presence," for example, from the appropriately titled *Shadow Train* (1982), he notes that ideas die almost as quickly as they spawn. Yet, Gery says, "it is precisely this experience of the fading and recalling, the grasping and letting go, that simulates the thinking of the nuclear age. His fragments of meaning orbit around each other like subatomic particles in a nucleus."

With Ashbery, however, it seems to me that we have gotten as far away from the *naming* of things as we can get. Which isn't to say I don't think there is a place for poems about nothingness, only that I'm not sure they advance the conversation on nuclearism. Destinerrance—by its

own non-definition—can't raise consciousness, can't conduct the energy
necessary to uproot denial.

———

ENERGY (noun) definition of:
1. the capacity of acting or being active, a usually positive spiritual
   force
2. vigorous exertion of power
3. usable power (as heat or electricity)
4. a fundamental entity of nature that is transferred between parts
   of a system in the production of physical change within the
   system

———

HUMAN SHADOW ON STONE

Sitting on the steps
in front of the bank,

waiting for it to open,
waiting for it

to anesthetize as holy—
brighter than day.

Stone steps whitened
by heat rays—

the place a person
rested remains

dark. Shaped charges
batter my heart:

Little Boy. Fat Man.
Pika don (Flash-

boom). As soon as
we name them—they die.

—poem by the author

—————

The protest poem, closely followed by the psychohistoric, is for me the most compelling of Gery's four categories, the most capable of producing physical change within the system, if poetry possibly can. In the others— the apocalyptic lyric poem and poems of destinerrance, especially after writing some of each—I sense a tendency toward shutting down—not wanting to think, let alone talk, about nuclear threat. In fact, three of Gery's four alternate terms for his categories—*against, through, from within,* and *around*—imply skirting around the issue, sweeping under the rug. Only *against,* the protest, feels adequately confrontational, physical.

—————

Today, I stumbled across another atomic acronym, LORCA, short for "Loss of Reactor Coolant Accident." According to the staff of Maine's Davistown Museum, part of whose mission is to increase awareness of environmental history:

> A LORCA occurs when a reactor vessel is breached or otherwise damaged and fuel assembly coolant (usually water) is no longer available. The continuing fission chain reaction can intensify resulting in the melting of fuel followed by the melting of the reactor vessel internals, bursting of pipes, and damage to pressure-operated relief valves. This is called a "serious core event." This is the worst-case-scenario accident for an operating nuclear reactor, other than vaporization.

—————

LORCA, example of:
LORCAs appear to be underway at three of the six Fukushima
Daiichi reactor units in Japan.

See also: Federico García, 1898–1936, Spanish poet and dramatist

—

    The Spanish poet Federico García Lorca developed the aesthetics
of *duende*, a goblin-like creature as depicted in Spanish mythology.
Duende, declared Lorca, is a force that terrorizes writers, urging them to
write because—to quote from his "Gacela of the Dark Death" (1955) as
translated by Robert Bly—"all must know I have not died." The *duende* is
a "bitter root" residing deep within the poet. The essence of creation, the
duende does not come at all unless it senses that death is a possibility.

> Seeking the *duende*, there is neither map nor discipline. We only
> know it burns the blood like powdered glass, that it exhausts, rejects
> all the sweet geometry we understand . . . . The arrival of the *duende*
> presupposes a radical change to all the old kinds of form . . .
> The *duende* never repeats itself, any more than the waves of the sea do
> in a storm.
>
>   —Federico García Lorca, "Theory & Function of the *Duende*,"
>   translated by A.S. Kline (2012)

—

On March 11, 2011, the *duende* visited itself upon Fukushima:

> After the first wave, survivors in Japan ventured down to the water's
> edge to survey who could be saved, only to be swept away by the
> second.
>
>   —Evan Osnos, "The Fallout," *The New Yorker* (2011)

—

Nineteen years after its "death," Yankee Rowe was resurrected in the world outside Western Massachusetts—depicted in Fukushima coverage, from *The New York Times* to *The Harvard Crimson*, as a turning point in the fate of aging nuclear power plants. The connection? In 1988, Yankee Rowe was selected by the industry as an ideal test case for those plants seeking relicensing when it requested an extension of the forty-year industry standard. In 2011, Japan's Fukushima Unit #1, constructed in 1967 and previously scheduled for shutdown, had just been granted a ten-year license renewal one month before the tsunami hit. It was the first in the disaster to fail.

Yankee Rowe ultimately withdrew its bid for relicensing, citing the cost of repairing its embrittled reactor pressure vessel, a condition which reduced its tolerance for cracks. The plant's owners maintained that their decision was based on economics. But Robert Pollard, a safety engineer with the Union of Concerned Scientists (UCS), said: "It's an economic decision forced upon them by a safety issue."

Seeking to avoid Rowe's fate, owners of Point Beach Nuclear Generating Station in Wisconsin, the next plant to seek relicensing, argued to the NRC that the license renewal process "examined aspects of plant operation beyond the scope of what was necessary . . . and the agency therefore ran the risk of making license renewal uneconomical." In response, the NRC relaxed its rules, and no longer requires applicants seeking renewal to prove compliance with the provisions of their current licenses.

According to former NRC commissioner David Lochbaum, who went on to a position as director of the Nuclear Safety Project at the Union of Concerned Scientists, "They [NRC] didn't want to find any more show-stoppers like they found at Yankee Rowe."

Since then, the rules have been relaxed to the extent that the NRC has granted every operating reactor's application to extend its original forty-year license by twenty more years and, at the time of this writing, eighty-one of one hundred US reactors currently operate on license renewals, well beyond their original design's forty-year lifespan which, according to Matthew Wald in *The New York Times*, was not even based on technical considerations but, rather, on the time span commonly used by utilities for accounting purposes.

WESTINGHOUSE PASTORAL

From the peak of Stump Sprouts, you can see
where the energy came into our lives.

Tan bald dome, crowning pool to pad,
grid to grille. Just east of Sherman Pond,

Indian paintbrush shades scrub grass
proud. People click on switches, trim

hedges, motor mowers. Life turns on
after shutdown. Weddings are thrown—

babies are born. Under the whispering
silk of row upon row of corn, spent

fuel rods sleep the sleep of apples.
Guns hover noses over seething concrete

casks. From the peak of the stump?
Ruined temples.

—poem by the author, reprinted by permission of
Negative Capability Press

In Charlemont (I think), after passing a bridge, we saw a very curious rock on the shore of the river, about twenty feet from the roadside. Clambering down the bank, we found it a complete arch, hollowed out of the solid rock, and as high as the arched entrance of an ancient church, which it might be taken to be, though considerably dilapidated and weather-worn. The water flows through it, though the rock afforded standing room, beside the pillars. It was really like the archway of an enchanted palace, all of which has vanished except the entrance, now only into nothingness and empty space.

—Nathaniel Hawthorne,
Passages from the American Notebooks (1838)

—

In September 2002, an al-Qaeda terrorist captured in Pakistan stated that the first targets considered for the 9/11 terrorist attack were nuclear reactors in the US. Later, they rejected the idea because of the threat of worldwide contamination. In July 2003, after pressure from CAN, Yankee Rowe's spent fuel storage finally moved from closely packed pools without adequate security to an interim dry cask storage system. A better solution, but one that nevertheless prevents future development of the site. Professor Mullin observes:

> Some antinuclear activists have proposed that the Rowe facility be left intact for decades to come, to permit the core's radioactivity to decline . . . . Interestingly, Rowe will then have a second "ghost" area added to the abandoned nineteenth-century Davis Village, whose 150 structures were ultimately demolished.

—

Davis Village, located in Rowe in the 1800s, was the United States' premier sulfur mine. The development of the mine came at a time when iron pyrite was just beginning to replace brimstone as a source of sulphuric acid. The Davis ore was particularly favored for its lack of arsenic. With Davis's death in 1905, maintenance of the mine shafts declined, and after several serious cave-ins, stopped in August 1911. Ghosttowns.com memorializes the mine as follows:

NAME: Davis Mine
COUNTY: Franklin
ROADS: 2WD
GRID: 1
CLIMATE: Lots of snow in the winter
REMAINS: 4 deep shafts, some sulphur ore, several foundations.
COMMENTS: This is a medium sulphur pyrite mining town in
Rowe, Massachusetts, started around 1880 and died about 1910. It is
on private property, so it's best to secure permission from the owner.

Nobody lives in there anymore.

———

NOVEMBER SACRAMENT

You said I would need to circle the seasons.
Perhaps you were right. Something has shifted.

I went back to the hospital's cerulean sixth floor
clutching mums for Mary, Lucy, and Vashan,

the nurses who saw you would not breathe for long.
One who stood by your bed, squeezed your toe, said:

Goodbye, Dennis. I guess you'll really hate me now.
That bloody tube—your crucifix.

I saw you rear up like a roped calf,
through the derelict door, left ajar.

But it kept you alive long enough
for one last pilgrimage, one last chance.

By chance, I pass the chapel. Voices float
me inside. *Father?*

God, we love you. You an awesome father.
You a mighty father. Lord have mercy.

Four seasons have passed. Another Thanksgiving.
It is right to give you thanks and praise.

—poem by the author, reprinted by permission of
Negative Capability Press

———

Paracelsus is thought to have been the first to have concocted an opium cocktail he labeled *laudanum* to ease pain in the very ill. As listed in the *London Pharmacopoeia* (1618), laudanum takes its name from the Latin verb *laudare*, meaning *to praise*. In addition to opium, it also contained saffron, castor, ambergris, musk, crushed pearls, and nutmeg.

The opiate administered to my father after we removed him from his artificial ventilator was the less poetic but more potent fentanyl, or "fent," as the medical professionals called it in shorthand. The tech explained that the drug would ease my father's pain, and that he would eventually overdose on it, causing hypoventilation, or cessation of breathing.

When the technician removed the tube from my father's body, his brow immediately became furrowed, but he did not open his eyes. My sisters, Denny, and I all held and stroked his hands and feet, determined to give him "a good death," periodically requesting that the tech administer more fent. *All things are poison and nothing is without poison. Only the dose makes it that a thing is not a poison. Alle Dinge sind Gift, und nichts ist ohne Gift; allein die dosis machts, daß ein Ding kein Gift sei.*

We knew my father had received his final "gift" when we heard him produce a belabored inhalation absent its counterpart.

———

PROXY

i.
I will answer forever to that unfinished sound:
rasping suck, then—

84

ii.
As when tulips come up too early in spring.
Fooled. Unfurling just halfway.

iii.
I rub your feet, whisper foolish things.
Just let go. You're free now. Fly.

Tape stretches over your mouth like wings
for eight days now—nine? In the end

Mother wants to fly in, say goodbye.
I watch her chide what's left of you

about the Thanksgiving you dropped
the turkey on the kitchen floor,

the time your new car rolled downhill.
This is how she loves. I know this, but still—

iv.
I excuse myself from what is left of you two:
her odd memories, your body no more

than an empty frame, the air sucked in, turned
with your own blood, sent out again.

Hypnotic as a hymn, overheard
on some gone Sunday. We sipped lemonade

in the dark. *The leaves are turning over,*
you say, as I think *it's going to rain.*

v.
We set our drinks on coasters. Rock mutely,
looking for stars. They unfurl in clusters. Pulse.

—poem by the author, reprinted by permission of
Negative Capability Press

A week or so after my father died, there were no leaves left to be seen on the paucity of trees overhanging my Brooklyn backyard. It was early December. I decided to transplant the Rose of Sharon to a sunnier location, where I assumed it would have a better chance to thrive. With the flora thinned, I had easy access to the stripling shrub and began to chip away at half-frozen earth with a cheap trowel.

Eyes blurred by tears, I stabbed dimly into the dirt, increasingly dismayed at the violence needed to excavate the extensive network of roots that had managed in just a few months to stitch themselves incisively to the soil. Then the tool broke, and it was just my fingers and my grief. It took a good hour, but I was finally able to pull the root ball, more or less intact, from the ground. With most of the root and a few smaller tendrils still attached, I pronounced it a successful surgery.

Exhausted from the dig, I decided to container the tree. I would re-site it in the ground come spring. However, when spring arrived and I looked for signs of life in the ever more symbolic plant, there weren't many to be found. A few tiny leaves sprouted, then, just as quickly, withered and died. In the perfect vision of hindsight, it occurred to me that, had I left the weed in its chosen spot, it probably would have done just fine.

LEARNING TO LEAVE THINGS ALONE

I see the cat quiver and point. A huddle of gray
feathers pulls into focus in the backyard corner:

head down, wings tucked, growing small and still
the flies have begun to take notice. I get a shoebox

and shoo them away. When I pick him up,
he does not struggle. So I dare to stroke the space

between his wings. Claws splay, striving to find
a foothold and his speckled breast flutters—

then one last valiant wing-stretch, tail rising
like a rudder. I set the box in a hanging planter,

empty, swayed by a late May breeze. Days later,
it occurred to me: Might the bird have preferred

to have died on familiar ground, among best-loved
colors, even with the flies pecking at his eyes?

—poem by the author, reprinted by permission of
Negative Capability Press

As the great scholar of grief, Elisabeth Kübler-Ross, says in *On Death and Dying* (1997):

> Dying becomes lonely and impersonal because the patient is often
> taken out of his familiar environment and rushed to an emergency
> room. . . . He slowly but surely is beginning to be treated like a thing.
> He is no longer a person.

My father's name was Dennis Kiernan. He shunned the use of his middle name because he shared it with his father, Roy, an ex-Army man turned alcoholic salesman of used cars. He refused to give me a middle name, too, deeming them worthless. His mother, Alice, was a painter who, in her own words, "designed a lot of ugly fabric that sold well" and Corningware's best-selling cookware pattern, "Spice O' Life."

Dennis was born in New York City and, at age eight, sent to Jay, Maine, to live with his maternal grandparents, after Roy, in an alcoholic rage, came after Alice with a carving knife. Though she was unharmed, it is maybe unsurprising that Dennis became a psychologist specializing in counseling children with profound emotional and physical challenges. In later life, he enjoyed a too-brief success with photography.

He enjoyed poetry, too. He read it—regularly—and even wrote it from time to time. In the hospital, I would read him poems from *The New Yorker*, and even though he would insist, in 2003, that Carter was president, and that it was mid-summer notwithstanding the bare trees, he easily recalled a poem's images and lines. What's more, he could paraphrase every poem I read to him, providing me with a literal reading during a time when I found almost everything impenetrable—especially poetry.

Another time I was his student: While a flute performance major at the University of Michigan in 1982, I wrote and mailed him some poems— poems, in hindsight, both literally and figuratively sophomoric. He sent me the following one in return, in beautiful penmanship and composed in what I only now recognize as perfect iambic dimeter except—and effectively—for the poem's final line:

STRUCTURE

for Lissa

I like to see
How things are made,
How twig joins branch
And stem sprouts blade.

I like to see
the petals fall,
Revealing pod
And shiny seed.

I like to see
The curve of earth
Through leafless woods
Upon the hill,

And know I'll smell
Arbutus soon
As certain as the plan.

—poem by Dennis Kiernan,
  reprinted by permission of
  the author's estate

———

STRUCTURE (noun) definition of:
1. the arrangement of particles or parts in a substance or body
2. the aggregate of elements of an entity in their relationships to
   each other
3. the arrangement of atoms in a molecule of a chemical compound
4. biology morphology; form

———

A CHEMISTRY OF PHANTOMS

If I were to tell you now what this place means—
it would be silty green—opaque jade, like
the river reflects lately, mingled with muffled

gunmetal signaling the start of hunting season.
Yesterday, the sighting of two white forest
creatures, the first a squirrel, white as night

snow—no, more like cream, it poured out
of the bramble. *Oh, my God,* I murmured,
and Chris angled his camera, catching

an improbable glimpse, too. The second
was barely a flicker of light, snuffed out
as fast as it grew, dissolving into the thicket,

half-cat, half-fox. I trilled for a minute
into the chilled wood-smoked air, hoping
that cat you loved but could never name—

Ginger, Galinger, or Linger—would appear.
She slipped into these lanky woods
one honey-crisp afternoon—a hawk,

some said, probably took her. Or perhaps
she tried to cross the river and failed,
the current shifting, like today's, swollen

to straining, post-Irene. See how the wrack
line brands the big rock? In Shelburne Falls,
she washed away decades of flowers

and the one good bookstore. And now,
a familiar hum, electric, particular—
of what, I don't know, perhaps

the steam cargo train or the new wind
turbine that turns lazily from Berkshire East,
on its own terms, in its own time.

While it should give me hope, and does, some
part of me (the bigger part, if I'm honest)
thinks *too little, too late.*

But the river still beckons, deeper than ever
I've seen it. Cold—no, cool, a salve
on a wound at this point in time in this place

on the planet, a day when Indian summer strikes
the eye like an arrow. Chris is inside, working
on his pictures, and I'm on the deck, finally writing

in longhand. Was it you? Those two flashes of white—
and if so, what's your message? Should we move,
live here? Knowing what I know, fearing what I fear?

Light glances off wind-spun spider webs,
strung between stalks—
lifting like ghosts from the bed of hosta.

—poem by the author, reprinted by permission of
Negative Capability Press

About the Author

Dennis Kiernan and Lissa Kiernan

photo by Chris Abramides

Lissa Kiernan was born the middle daughter of three to Claudette (Viau) and Dennis Kiernan. Raised primarily in Athol, Massachusetts, she spent her eleventh year in Nashville, Tennessee. A classically trained pianist and flutist, she began her higher education as a music performance major in Ann Arbor, Michigan, before discovering her passion for poetry and writing. She worked as an *au pair* in Paris, France, before returning home to finish her BA in English at the University of Massachusetts, Amherst. Upon graduation, she moved to New York City, where she settled in Brooklyn and, in 1989, married her husband, Chris Abramides.

She was employed at various times as a typesetter, transcriber, jewelry designer, legal secretary, salesperson, and consumer relations representative while earning her MA in Media Studies from The New School, completed in 1998. Since then, she has worked as a web producer and, after earning her MFA from the Stonecoast Creative Writing program in 2011, as a poetry teacher.

Her first full-length volume of poetry, *Two Faint Lines in the Violet* (Negative Capability Press, 2014), was a *Foreword Reviews'* INDIEFAB Book of the Year Award finalist, as well as a finalist for the Julie Suk Award for Best Poetry Book by an Independent Press.

Kiernan founded and directs the Poetry Barn, a literary center based in New York's Catskill Park, sponsoring workshops, readings, craft talks, and book arts for all ages. *Glass Needles & Goose Quills* is her second book and first book of prose.

Acknowledgments

I am indebted to many people who supported my desire to bring this book into the world. I would like to thank Nicole Cooley, who served as mentor as I began to write this story and who encouraged me to see it to print. I would also like to thank Jeanne Marie Beaumont and Ted Deppe for helping me navigate through the creation of many of the difficult-to-voice poems included herein.

I am infinitely grateful to Marcia Gagliardi, my high school English teacher, who encouraged my nascent writing urge and continued to advocate for it throughout the years, culminating in her agreeing to publish my book "in a heartbeat," never suspecting, I imagine, that the process would take three years. She is a pioneering nuclear activist, an exacting editor, and an astutely discriminating reader. I could not have asked for a more perfect publisher.

Likewise, I am obliged to Marcia's daughter, Jane Gagliardi, for whom I once babysat and who now serves as Associate Professor of Psychiatry & Behavioral Sciences and of Medicine at Duke University School of Medicine. Having an academic physician-educator willing to make a statement about the merits of this book was an unexpected gift and a huge boost at a point where my courage and confidence were flagging.

I am deeply appreciative of Keith Harmon Snow and Deb Katz for their brave and authoritative investigative and activist work and for generously allowing me to reprint some of their most powerful and influential statements. I am also beholden to John Gery, whose groundbreaking scholarly research on the nuclear canon facilitated my increased understanding of the invaluable contributions of my forebears.

I cannot neglect to thank my husband, Chris Abramides, who no doubt felt neglected at many points during this book's evolution as I struggled and fought again and again to get it right. He gave me the greatest luxuries of all—time and space—along with his implicit endorsement, all the while serving as an excellent sounding board for the literate layperson who might be inherently skeptical about a number of the book's allegations.

I thank my talented and lovely musician mother, Claudette (Viau) Kiernan, for endowing me, among other things, through years of instruction, patience, love, and practice, with what I would like to think is a somewhat refined musical ear, and I am thankful for my sisters, Michelle Kiernan and Suzanne Perkinson, and their husbands, James Johnston and Terry Perkinson, for their love, support, and artistic encouragement throughout the years.

I offer heartfelt gratitude to my late father's partner, Denny Fuller, for doing everything within his power to care for my father during the course of his battle with brain cancer, a daunting and often thankless responsibility.

And last, but surely not least, I thank my dear father, Dennis Kiernan, for teaching me to make haste slowly and to be true to my own voice.

Comments on the Text

"Disposal" juxtaposes text from "Nuke Trainspotting Warns of Drive-by Dosing" (Michael Steinberg, *The Prism,* March 2004) with "Yankee Rowe waste materials are traveling over Vermont roads" (Carolyn Lorie, *Brattleboro Reformer*, March 2004).

"Facility" incorporates text from *Source Water Assessment and Protection (SWAP) Report for Yankee Atomic Electric Company*, as well as a popular English-language nursery rhyme having a Roud Folk Song Index number of 11318.

In "Eclogue on Decommissioning," the phrase "in much the same way a glass dish, hot from the oven would crack if doused in cold water" is borrowed from a Union of Concerned Scientists Fact Sheet accompanying a petition from the New England Coalition on Nuclear Pollution (NECNP) to the Nuclear Regulatory Commission (NRC) for an immediate shutdown of Yankee Rowe Atomic.

The title "Atoms for Peace" and the sentence "I feel the need to speak today in a language that in a sense is new" are borrowed from a speech delivered by President Dwight D. Eisenhower to the UN General Assembly in New York City on December 8, 1953.

The phrase "sleep the sleep of the apples" in "Westinghouse Pastoral" is borrowed from Robert Bly's translation of Federico García Lorca's "Gacela de la Muerte Oscura" or "Gacela of the Dark Death."

The excerpt from Judith Vollmer's "Yucca Mountain Sequence" corrects the name of the river from Connecticut to Deerfield.

Permissions

Permissions are shown in order of appearance of the relevant poem or other citation in the text.

Marie Cartier, "The Seasons Will Change," reprinted with permission of the author.

Paul Zimmer, excerpt from "But Bird" from *Big Blue Train*. Copyright © 1993 by Paul Zimmer. Reprinted with the permission of The Permissions Company, Inc., on behalf of University of Arkansas Press, www.uapress.com.

Hillman, Brenda. "[half-tractate]" from *Pieces of Air in The Epic* © 2005 by Brenda Hillman. Reprinted by permission of Wesleyan University Press.

"The Closing of the Yankee Rowe Nuclear Power Plant: The Impact on a New England Community." Mullin, John R. and Zenia Kotval. *Journal of the American Planning Association,* 1939-0130, Vol. 63, Issue 4. 1997. Reprinted by permission of Taylor & Francis Ltd, http://www.tandf. co.uk/journals.

Copyright © 1979 by Susan Griffin, from *Woman and Nature: The Roaring Inside Her*. Reprinted by permission of Counterpoint.

"Sloan-Kettering" from SLOAN-KETTERING: POEMS by Abba Kovner, translation copyright © 2002 by the Estate of Abba Kovner. Used by permission of Schocken Books, an imprint of the Knopf Doubleday Publishing Group, a division of Penguin Random House LLC. All rights reserved.

Vollmer, Judith. "REACTOR" © 2004 by the Board of Regents of the University of Wisconsin System. Reprinted by permission of The University of Wisconsin Press.

Resources and Works Cited

Bloom, Susan L. "Emotional Anesthesia: The Double Bind for Doctors," *The Psychotherapy Review* 1(2): 63–63, 1999.

Cartier, Marie. "The Seasons Will Change." Peace Newsletter, August, 1982.

Castle, William B., Katherine R. Drinker and Cecil K. Drinker, "Necrosis of the Jaw in Radium Workers," *Journal of Industrial Hygiene*. August 1925.

Citizens Awareness Network. *The Carcinogenic, Mutagenic, Teratogenic and Transmutational Effects of Tritium.* Ed. Deb Katz. April 1994 (updated January 2001).

_____. *The Radioactivist*. Ed. Deb Katz. May 2005.

_____. *The Radioactivist*. Ed. Deb Katz. October 2008.

_____. "Decommissioning–Nuclear Wars of the '90s." Ed. Deb Katz. 19 March 2004.

Crittenden, Chris. "Ecofeminism Quote." Email to the author. September 2010.

"Davis Mine." Ghosttowns.com. n.d.

DuBois, B. *Passionate Scholarship: Notes on Values, Knowing, and Method in Feminist Social Science.* London: Routledge & Kegan Paul, 1983.

"Fukushima Daiichi Nuclear Disaster." Davistown Museum, Liberty, Maine. 17 March 2011.

"General Information." Yankeerowe.com. Yankee Nuclear Power Plant. n.d.

Griffin, Susan. *Woman and Nature: The Roaring Inside Her.* New York: Harper & Row Publishers, 1978.

Harmon Snow, Keith. "Nuclear Poisons." *Valley Advocate Newspapers.* 6–12 July 1995.

———. "The Hottest Swimming Holes in the Whole Damned River." Allthingspass.com.

———. "Nuclear Apocalypse in Japan." ConsciousBeingAlliance.com.

Hillman, Brenda. "[half-tractate]." *Pieces of Air in The Epic.* Middletown: Wesleyan University Press, 2005. Reprinted by permission.

Kiernan, Dennis. "Happy Birthday." Email to the author. September 2003.

———. Letter to the author. October 1986.

Kolbert, Elizabeth. "Near Old Nuclear Plant, Town Keeps the Faith." *The New York Times,* 20 July 1991.

Kovner, Abba. *Sloan-Kettering: Poems.* New York: Schocken Books, 2002.

Kübler-Ross, Elisabeth. *On Death and Dying.* New York: Scribner, 1997.

Leonard, Elizabeth Ann Dermody. *Convicted Survivors: The Imprisonment of Battered Women Who Kill.* Albany; State University of New York Press, 1997.

Levertov, Denise. *Selected Poems.* Ed. Paul A. Lacey. New York: New Directions Publishing Corporation, 2002.

_____. "On the Edge of Darkness, What is Political Poetry?" *Light Up the Cave.* New York: New Directions Publishing, 1981.

Lifton, Robert Jay and Richard Falk. *Indefensible Weapons: The Political and Psychological Case against Nuclearism.* New York: Basic Books, 1982.

"List of locations in *The Simpsons.*" Wikipedia. 2010. Wikimedia Foundation, Inc.

Lorca, Federico García. "Theory & Play of the *Duende*," translated by A. S. Kline. 2007. Poetryintranslation.com.

Lorie, Carolyn. "Yankee Rowe waste materials are traveling over Vermont roads." *Brattleboro Reformer,* 9 March 2004.

Malley, Marjorie. *Radioactivity: A History of a Mysterious Science.* New York: Oxford University Press, 2011.

Massachusetts Department of Environmental Protection. *Source Water Assessment and Protection (SWAP) Report for Yankee Atomic Electric.* 24 October 2003.

_____. Department of Public Health. *Assessment of Cancer Incidence and Down Syndrome Prevalence in the Deerfield River Valley, Massachusetts. Boston.* 1997.

Merriam-Webster Online Dictionary. 2010. Merriam-Webster Online.

Mullin, John R. and Zenia Kotval. "The Closing of the Yankee Rowe Nuclear Power Plant: The Impact on a New England Community." *Journal of the American Planning Association*, 1939-0130, Vol. 63, Issue 4. 1997.

Nichols, Lynn. "Town Spotlight: Rowe." Valley Viewpoint. 19 March 2004. Print.

Noriega, Kim. *Name Me.* Ed. Cecilia Woloch. Fortunate Daughter Press, 2010.

"Nuclear Plant Owners Warned to Check for Cracked Turbines," *The Argus-Press*. Print. 30 March 1980.

Osnos, Evan. "The Fallout." *The New Yorker.* 17 October 2011.

"Poetic Form: Found Poem." The Academy of American Poets (poets. org).

"Poverty raises brain tumor risk, study finds." Reuters Limited, 2004.

Rukeyser, Muriel. *The Life of Poetry*. Ashfield, MA: Paris Press, 1996.

_____. *The Collected Poems of Muriel Rukeyser*. Ed. Janet E. Kaufman and Anne F. Herzog with Jan Heller Levi, Pittsburgh: University of Pittsburgh Press, 2005.

Shapiro, Lynn. "Sloan-Kettering." *Rattle #26*, Winter 2006.

Snyder, Gary. *Turtle Island*. New York: New Directions, 1974.

Solnit, Rebecca. *Savage Dreams: A Journey Into the Landscape Wars of the American West*. Berkeley and Los Angeles: University of California Press, 1999.

Sontag, Susan. *Styles of Radical Will*. New York: Macmillan, 2002.

Steinberg, Michael. "Nuke Trainspotting Warns of Drive-by Dosing." *The Prism*. May 1997.

Thomas, Lewis. *The Medusa and the Snail*. New York: Penguin, 1979.

Thomson, Philip. *The Grotesque*. London: Methuen, 1972.

United States. National Institutes of Health Clinical Trials. *Assessment of Comskil Training Through Videorecording and Patient Surveys*. 21 July 2009.

Vollmer, Judith. *Reactor*. Madison, WI. The University of Wisconsin Press. 2004.

Wald, Matthew. "A-Plant Shut Down, Ending Industry's Test Case." *The New York Times,* 27 Feb. 1992.

Wilbur, Richard. *Responses: Prose Pieces 1953–1976.* Ashland: Story Line Press, 1999.

Williams, William Carlos. "Asphodel, That Greeny Flower." *Asphodel, That Greeny Flower and Other Love Poems.* New York: New Directions Publishing Corporation, 1955.

CPSIA information can be obtained
at www.ICGtesting.com
Printed in the USA
FFOW03n2306200917
40085FF